Celebrating 25 Years

T0245673

SACRED SPACE

Retreats & Reflections for Daily Life

from the website www.sacredspace.ie
Prayer from the Irish Jesuits

LOYOLAPRESS.
A JESUIT MINISTRY
Chicago

LOYOLA PRESS.
A JESUIT MINISTRY
www.loyolapress.com

This edition of **Sacred Space: Retreats & Reflections for Daily Life** is published by Loyola Press by arrangement with Messenger Publications, Dublin, Ireland.

Scripture quotations are taken from the *New Revised Standard Version Updated Edition*. Copyright © 2021 National Council of Churches of Christ in the United States of America. Used by permission. All rights reserved worldwide.

Cover art credit: Nebula Cordata/Getty Images

ISBN: 978-0-8294-5935-7
Library of Congress Control Number: 2024939791

Printed in the United States of America.
24 25 26 27 28 29 30 31 32 Versa 10 9 8 7 6 5 4 3 2 1a

Contents

Sacred Space Prayer

*Bless all who worship you, almighty God,
from the rising of the sun to its setting:
from your goodness enrich us,
by your love inspire us,
by your Spirit guide us,
by your power protect us,
in your mercy receive us,
now and always.*

Foreword by
Bishop Alan McGuckian SJ

In 1998 the web was just beginning to become widely used in Ireland, and I was in charge of Jesuit Communications. I heard Terry Prone, the doyenne of Irish communications, say, 'Everybody is wasting money setting up websites that do nothing for anybody. If you're going to have a website make sure that it gives people something they want or need.' That set me thinking; what do we Jesuits have to offer that people might want? Almost immediately I had a picture of myself sometime previously in a group doing a guided meditation on a Scripture scene. There I was, eyes closed, listening to someone speaking, then sitting in silence contemplating what I'd heard; then the leader spoke again and moved my contemplation forward; then the leader read a scene from the Scriptures and left the group time in silence to sit with the scene and speak to God about it.

I knew right away that anyone could give themselves the same kind of experience with a mouse in their hand, moving slowly from one screen to the next, following the movement of a guided prayer session and taking lots of time for silent prayer along the way.

I had the idea very clear in my head, and providence intervened by sending Peter Scally SJ to work with me in the Jesuit Communication Centre in Dublin on a two-year placement before his theology studies. Peter had the creativity and the technological skill to make it happen. He bought a book on website design and, with the book in one hand and a mouse in the other, he brought the first Sacred Space to life in time for Ash Wednesday 1999.

As we approached the big launch day we had a lot of fun getting publicity. The idea of anyone PRAYING in front of a computer seemed so novel and utterly outlandish, and we played it up in our press releases. Media outlets were hooked and we got great coverage in most of the national newspapers. Peter and I had to divide the invitations to talk on radio shows in Ireland, the UK and Vatican Radio.

By the time Ash Wednesday was over we knew that over 1,000 people had logged on to Sacred Space to pray. And then the reactions started flowing in. People were really praying and more than that they had a deep sense that they were united with a great community of others praying along with them.

Then the feedback became deeper and deeper. People were being moved in powerful and unexpected ways and wanted to share it with us. Two stories are etched in my memory. One person wrote, 'I have not been inside a Catholic church in three years, since the day when I was crawling among the living and the dead along the floor of a church in Rwanda during the genocide. For the first time I have been able to pray with you at Sacred Space.' That person had found a sense of community in prayer with Sacred Space that was a stepping stone out of darkness and back to full communion. Another deeply poignant message, 'I have not been to Mass with my local community in two years since my little girl died. In recent times I have prayed at Sacred Space and now I feel ready to go back to Mass for the first time next Sunday.'

Those two very dramatic stories conjured up the image of Sacred Space giving people who didn't feel strong enough to gather with others physically the opportunity to join in community prayer as if from behind a pillar where they felt safe. It was obvious that grace was at work in their hearts and the bonds of community were being strengthened even in the apparent isolation of their own room.

At the time it was new and exciting. Immediately I decided that we would make Sacred Space available in Irish too. We set to work and on St Patrick's Day, just a few weeks later, tearmann.com was born and people had the choice between praying in English and Irish. Within days a woman called Sofia Andrade wrote saying that she loved praying in this way but would like to do it in her native Portuguese. She was a part of Christian Life Communities in Portugal and she undertook to ensure that their group would do the necessary translations. In the months and years that followed more and more languages came on board. I've been away from it for a long time, and I've lost count. It all feels like a wonderful Pentecost, a steady outpouring of grace and so many people have stepped in and helped channel it in Dublin and all over the world.

And then, Sacred Space became a book! I never saw that coming. It was a wonderful Australian lady, whose name I can't remember, who arrived in our office saying that many people would prefer to pray with a book in their hand rather than a mouse. She was a publisher in Australia and, even though we were sceptical, we encouraged her to give it a go. How right she was, and now you are sitting reading *Sacred Space: Retreats & Reflections for Daily Life* for the year 2024, our silver anniversary. It's all a work of the Holy Spirit and you are part of it.

As Sacred Space was coming into being we had a deep sense that St Ignatius of Loyola was in the process. His experience of being led in prayer was guiding us along the way. Read on and learn a little bit about how God led him on an inner journey. Ignatius had a powerful conviction that God, who speaks to us through the Scriptures and the Church's tradition, meets us and changes us in the very depths of our own being. When we pray we put ourselves into God's presence—the Word of God *is* the presence of God—and we trust that his Holy Spirit will act in us, move us, change us. Often, if we pay attention, we can recognise God at work in the bits and pieces of our daily round and we can cooperate more intentionally. (For more on this read the section on the Examen.) Sometimes, we don't see what God is doing; we simply trust that when we are in his presence God is at work and that is all that matters.

Let me go back to the beginning and the novelty, and seeming absurdity, of praying in front of a computer. It is true that people can become very isolated in front of computers; they can have a false sense of connection. The success of Sacred Space then highlights the fact that prayer always draws us into community; it unites us with Jesus and he brings us into the life of the Blessed Trinity. Further, even if we are not adverting to it, prayer unites us with Mary and all the saints and with all the other brothers and sisters of Jesus throughout the world. I pray that, through Sacred Space, you may experience the closeness of God and your closeness to the 'great cloud of witnesses' gathered around God's throne.

+Alan McGuckian SJ
Bishop of Raphoe

Introduction to the Adventure of Ignatian Spirituality

Ignatius of Loyola (1491–1556) was one of those specially gifted friends of God who has left a spiritual legacy that endures. He was a charismatic teacher and mentor for those seeking to deepen their relationship with God. For many people during his lifetime and since his death, he has embodied a distinctively holistic way of living the Christian faith. Today his life experiences still speak to ours. His faith-vision engages us as, in some mysterious way, it transcends the centuries. But we also know Ignatius as a flawed human being, one who like us experienced moral failures and psychological problems. He always saw himself as in need of God's mercy. The spirituality that we call Ignatian is nothing if not realistic. It is authentically human even as it entices us to taste of the divine. And it is available to everyone: young and old, women and men, ordained and non-ordained.

Ignatius lived in a century of great change. The Renaissance was fostering developments in art and culture, and was transforming the approach to education throughout Europe. The Protestant Reformations—there was more than one—introduced new ideas into theology and spirituality, and challenged the authority of the Roman Church.

xii   Introduction to the Adventure of Ignatian Spirituality

The voyages of discovery led to a vast expanding
of people's imaginative horizons, brought immense
wealth back to Europe from the recently conquered
lands, and opened a new era of missionary work for
the Church. We have learned to pay more attention to the historical context of saints' lives than we
may have done in the past. The turbulence of the
sixteenth century affected Ignatius's thinking, his
choices, his spirituality, and therefore his holiness.
He would have been a different person, a different saint, if he had lived in the ninth or nineteenth
century. But under God's providence he walked
this earth at a particular time (not any time), in a
specific historical era (not some other era), meeting
certain people (and not others). It was in these concrete circumstances that he sought and found God,
and that he grew in intimacy with him. We cannot
turn Ignatius into a twenty-first century person. We
cannot simply imitate him in every aspect of his life.
Likewise, knowing historical facts about Ignatius
will not of itself contribute much to our own growth.
If we want to learn from Ignatius we need to get
inside his experience, so far as that is possible. We
need to discover how God worked in him.

Ignatius's story is about movement, about journeying, about a search, about exploration. God accompanies him along many paths, sometimes nudging

him forward, sometimes restraining him. These paths are, quite literally, the roads of Europe—not forgetting the Mediterranean Sea—that brought him to Montserrat, Manresa, Barcelona, the Holy Land, Alcalá, Salamanca, Paris, Venice and Rome. Over years this will see Ignatius change, develop and grow into the person that God wants him to be. Neither does the starting point of either the outer or the inner journey give any clue as to where it will end. Convalescing in his family's castle in Loyola, Ignatius can have no idea that the final years of his life will be spent in Rome.

Ignatius's paths are also metaphorical or figurative, however, symbolising his inner journey. This journey begins with 'a man given to worldly vanities, and having a vain and overpowering desire to gain renown,' and it ends with a man whose 'ease in finding God was always increasing, now more than ever in his entire life. At whatever time or hour he wanted to find God, he found him.' God led Ignatius from being an ambitious, boisterous knight, filled with dreams of chivalry, to becoming a person whose only desire was 'to praise, reverence and serve God our Lord.'

All Christians are pilgrims. We are on a journey, like Abraham who 'set out, not knowing where he was going' (Hebrews 11:8). Abraham is praised for his faith, which in this context is synonymous with trust. He trusted the God who had called him. He did not need to know the destination. It was enough that God was with him. So too with Ignatius, who trusted that God would not desert him, abandon him, or allow him to go too far astray. Both his story and that of Abraham invite us to a similar trust. Life will always bring changes, gains and losses, clarity and confusion. Through it all we are encouraged to leave ourselves in the hands of God, to allow him to write our own personal story.

The Jesuit Cardinal Carlo Maria Martini, who died in 2012, was asked what message Ignatius might have for the third millenium. He answered, 'I think there is one especially salient message Ignatius can give us: the great value of interiority. I mean by this everything that has to do with the sphere of the heart, of deep intentionality, of decisions made from within.'

Interiority is precisely the word that I too would use. Self-knowledge, purifying the heart, the inner journey, finding one's centre, the still point—these and other similar ideas and images have constantly appeared in the Christian spiritual tradition. In the Christian experience all of this is linked with prayer—not just saying prayers but praying unceasingly, really becoming people of prayer. One might even paraphrase Socrates and say, 'The prayer-less life is not worth living.'

The argument for interiority today is not simply that it has been a continuous part of the Christian spiritual tradition. It is also that interiority is the antidote to much that is insidiously destructive in our contemporary society. The secularisation of culture, the frantic pace of life, the pressures of competition, the seductiveness of consumerism, the mind-controlling influence of both social and mass media, the intrusiveness of advertising—these and other influences mould our way of living. Busyness replaces reflectiveness, anxiety replaces contentment, and the craving for instant gratification replaces thoughtful attention to long-term goals. Even the quality of our most precious relationships is frequently put at risk. We are drawn to live superficially, on the surface of things, losing touch with our deeper and more authentic selves. We may not individually have succumbed to all these dangers, yet few would deny experiencing a struggle to 'live out of our centre' and to act in accordance with our highest ideals and deepest desires. These desires may even remain hidden or buried, lost from consciousness. 'What do you really want?' is often a surprisingly difficult question for people to answer spontaneously and with conviction.

We may also be deceived by the apparent good. Ignatius was convinced that good people are not likely to be deceived or led astray by blatant or gross temptations. Instead they have to be lured by a suggestion that either appears to be good, or really is good but not appropriate at this particular time. He writes in the *Spiritual Exercises*,

It is characteristic of the evil angel, who takes on the appearance of an angel of light, to enter by going along the same way as the devout soul, and then to exit by his own way with success for himself. That is, he brings good and holy thoughts attractive to such an upright soul and then strives little by little to get his own way, by enticing the soul over to his own hidden deceits and evil intentions [*SE*, 332].

This quotation addresses a situation where the temptation itself, and the best ways of dealing with it, are both extremely subtle. The underlying presupposition is clear, however. We recognise the temptation for what it is, we discover what is really happening, only if we are exercising interiority. Without self-awareness, and a sensitivity to how God and the evil spirit are working in us, we will be deceived.

The practice that Ignatius proposes to help us grow in interiority is the Consciousness Examen. An older generation knew this as the Examination of Conscience, where we looked back on the day—or some other period of time—and sought to discover where and how we had sinned and offended God.

This led to an expression of sorrow or regret, followed by a purpose of amendment. This exercise served many people well. A closer look at what is found in the *Spiritual Exercises*, however, reveals a more expansive approach. The shift from the word 'conscience' to 'consciousness' is the key that allows us to see the difference.

Conscience is the moral sense that we possess what enables us to distinguish right from wrong. The Examination of Conscience tended to focus on sin and the occasions of sin, on failure to obey the law of God, and on our need to be forgiven. This is not left aside in the Consciousness Examen but it becomes part of something bigger and more positive. Focusing on consciousness opens up the many ways in which we can become sensitive to the presence or absence of God in our lives. As we allow the day—or whatever period of time we are 'examining'—to pass before our inner eyes, we try to become aware of the situations, the events, the people where we found God, and those other situations, events and people where it was difficult to find him. We can pause in thanksgiving when God's presence was palpable, and pause in sorrow when we missed, ignored or did not appreciate that presence.

In activating our conscience, we mainly make use of our powers of reasoning, enlightened by faith.

Consciousness, however, allows us to explore the whole area of affectivity, our inner world of feelings and emotions, including the world of our imagination. We learn to notice our changing moods and other subjective movements, the images that surface—whether they attract or repel us—and to take this inner world seriously. In time we discover how rich this world is and, through discernment, how God is present and active in the mix. The examination of conscience has a slightly different emphasis. Since it deals primarily with sin and the occasions of sin, most attention is given to actions that are freely carried out. Consciousness, on the other hand, includes a range of spontaneous, 'non-free' movements, emotional reactions over which we have no control. This is part of the messiness of life. But God is as much in this swirling, unpredictable mingling of spontaneities as in our most rational thinking. Once we recognise this, we are on the way to discerning and interpreting how God is leading us and guiding our lives. The whole adventure begins when we answer the call to interiority.

Adapted from Brian O'Leary SJ
God Ever Greater: Exploring Ignatian Spirituality

ADVENT

Advent

Welcome to the first season of the Church's year, Advent. In the Christian calendar, Advent covers roughly the four weeks before Christmas, starting in late November or early December. Advent, however, is not simply a countdown to Christmas. Rather, we might think of this season as a signpost, marking our path, lighting our way, pointing to something beyond itself. Yes, it is a time of preparation for our celebration of the birth of Jesus, but it also marks a new Church year and a time to start over in our relationship with God and with others.

During the next few weeks, we will meet John the Baptist preparing the way for Jesus. We will meet Mary as she looks ahead to the birth of her baby, and Elizabeth as she welcomes and celebrates this amazing news. In many ways, these characters are an unlikely bunch—a marginalised, pregnant young woman; an older woman unexpectedly pregnant, and an eccentric wilderness preacher—but we read that they are all 'filled with the Holy Spirit'. They are the first witnesses to Jesus' coming into the world, and we follow their stories as they announce him to others.

During Advent, we are invited to a real encounter with Jesus. It is a time to wake up and to rediscover our joy in life. It is a time to practise the words of Mary, 'Let it be', and to be open to what adventures may come our way. We become more aware of God's presence in the hidden places of our world, in ourselves and in the people around us. Can we be signposts lighting the path for others? At this busy time of year, we are often caught up in the frantic joys, and sometimes struggles, of the season. The lead-up to Christmas evokes different emotions and memories for each of us. As we enter this new season and new Church year, it is important to take some time to check in with ourselves. The gospel texts offer us the opportunity to go back to the beginning and enter fully into these Spirit-filled days when the advent of Jesus, the light of the world, is so eagerly anticipated.

Tríona Doherty and Jane Mellet,
The Deep End: A Journey with the Sunday Gospels in the Year of Matthew

Advent Reflections

Season of Waiting

Advent is the annual season of waiting. We wait for the same reason every year, and we are certain that the One we await—a person, Jesus, Son of God—will arrive on time. Yet we find that the waiting is new each year, as Jesus is ever new. Maybe we don't like the waiting, or maybe we enter enthusiastically into Advent, which in some countries now starts in October. Maybe we are happy to wait in patience and quiet.

Some wait actively, reminding themselves each day with prayer or reflection as to why they wait. As Pope Francis says in *Let Us Dream*, our waiting is with the head (thinking about Advent), the heart (feeling with the season) and feet (doing something for others each day).

There's a richness in waiting. I'm impatient, but I find sometimes that when I relax into waiting, something good happens for me. Whether it's waiting for a bus or a plane, or queueing in a shop, I notice different things about people or even new colours in the sky. I notice how I am in myself, and, like in waiting for sleep, I may make sense of the stresses of the day. Waiting in many ways is a good thing for us.

We wait also to notice where and how God is in our lives. This waiting is often compared to the watchman who waits, noticing all that is happening around him. He's on a height to see the surrounding world. Advent can be our hill or mountain. Each day we gather something new about God, ourselves and the world.

The way we wait affects how we celebrate and enjoy Christmas. The way we wait may grow in us a new realisation that everything about God, and especially God's Son, is worth our waiting. We wait for the Lord, because his day is near. Thanks be to God!

Donal Neary SJ,
The Messenger Advent Booklet

Tidying the Room

We live in a world torn asunder by hatred, suspicion, bigotry and countless attributes that divide rather than unite, hurt rather than heal, and literally kill rather than give life. We can become numbed in the face of much of this, not least when it's on a massive scale and somewhat removed from us. Too easily we can blame or look for scapegoats. Too easily we can discriminate or brand others. Too easily we can withdraw into some sort of inner smugness that all is well in our house—my house. Is it?

Though we may not be killers or assassins, there is always the possibility that we are killing other people's spirits or darkening their world through bitterness or resentment, jealousy or hatred. We would never stand over the taking of life, and we recoil from violence, but at a subtle level, we might well consign others to a living death by ignoring or neglecting them. Maybe our words drive arrows into the heart of another. What we say about people could well add to their pain and exploit their vulnerability.

In these Advent days, having looked at tidying the room, we may worthily welcome our sacred guest, as the call to be builders of peace is real, urgent and essential. Taking an honest look into our own rooms, is there anyone that would not be welcome?

Is there anyone we've not spoken to or that we hold a grudge against? Is there even the slightest possibility of picking up the pieces and re-establishing contact? If you can at all, maybe now's the time.

Vincent Sherlock,
Let Advent Be Advent

The Feast of the Immaculate Conception

On the eve of the Feast of the Immaculate Conception, at 11:31 pm on 7 December 2022, little Ali entered this world. His mother, Fatima, gave birth to Ali in a small medical clinic on board the *Geo Barents*, a search and rescue vessel chartered by Médecins Sans Frontières (MSF) in the Mediterranean. Fatima had attempted to make the difficult journey from Libya with her three children, while heavily pregnant with Ali. It was a difficult labour, compounded by the trauma of the possible separation of the family: Fatima and Ali were to be taken by helicopter for postnatal medical treatment but Fatima's other two children were initially not allowed to enter that particular country.

To most of us the situation of Fatima and Ali is unthinkable, yet it is the story of millions of displaced families. There is a perception out there that asylum seekers choose to travel to other countries for economic reasons or because they just feel like it. The stark reality is that they are often fleeing for their lives, lives that are destroyed by the effects of climate change such as drought, famine, conflict for resources and many other related issues. They have no choice but to leave their homes and communities in order to survive. Thankfully, after hours of negotiation, Fatima's family was not split up and they were granted asylum along with 249 other passengers from this boat. It was a fraught start to little Ali's life.

Mary knew the fear and uncertainty of bringing a baby into a lonely, hostile situation. We remember today all mothers who give birth in difficult circumstances, particularly those who have been displaced or separated from family and support. We think of Mary, who entered the mystery of motherhood with bravery, and who reminds us that we are called to solidarity with all mothers and families, particularly those in crisis.

Tríona Doherty and Jane Mellet,
*The Deep End: A Journey with the Sunday Gospels
in the Year of Mark*

A Shy God

'And behold the Lord passed by, and a great and strong wind rent the mountains, and broke in pieces the rocks before the Lord, but the Lord was not in the wind, and after the end an earthquake, and after the earthquake a fire, and after the fire a still small voice.' (1 Kings 19:11–12)

This piece from the Book of Kings provides an illuminating insight into God's revelatory activity: God came not in a whirlwind but in a still, small voice.

Such a model allows us to see God present in the nature of all things and puts the onus on us to discern this presence. God's actions are hidden, because they are constant and because God acts within everything.

Just as we are never conscious of air, because God's presence is always around us, we never notice it. The journey of faith is a gift of a loving God who takes the first step and waits patiently, silently, almost shyly for the human response.

Life is a vocation, a call to seek this shy God.

This shy God did not come into the world with bells and thunder. When I was a young boy I sought God by looking up—trying to see if I could find God through some break in the sky. Today when I look for God I look down, not up, because I find

God in small things. As Pope Francis has said, we find the extraordinary in the ordinary.

The search for God this Advent requires us to look down. In doing so we follow the example of God. This shy God chose to come among us not in a palace or in a busy street but to become small and be born in a manger in the form of a helpless baby.

Advent is a time to remind ourselves of the many contradictions at the heart of our faith. This most powerful presence chose to be manifest in powerlessness.

As we prepare to celebrate the moment the Word became flesh our faith needs deepening. Ours is a faith that sincerely accepts the darkness surrounding the search for more light. Consequently, Advent is a time of loving adoration, a true act of supernatural hope and of loving surrender to this shy God.

This shy God reminds us this Advent that life is about relationships, not things. The greatest joy comes from good relationships—the greatest sorrow and suffering come not from loss of job or property but from broken and betrayed relationships. All relationships of love are rooted in the love this shy God has for all of us.

John Scally,
Waiting in Joy: An Advent Journey

Advent Retreat

A retreat in Advent helps us to look forward to Christmas and a new year, but it's also an opportunity to look back reflectively on how the past year has been for us, what we've endured but also what we've learned, how we've coped and, hopefully, how we've grown and adapted.

In Luke's Gospel Simeon prophesies to Mary and Joseph in the Temple that their child 'is destined for the falling and the rising of many in Israel'. He will be a sign of contradiction, 'so that the inner thoughts of many will be revealed' (Luke 2:34–35). Later in the same gospel Jesus tells the crowd, 'Nothing is covered up that will not be uncovered, and nothing secret that will not become known' (Luke 12:2). Difficult times reveal the vulnerability and, at times, the hypocrisy of many of the systems on which our societies depend. They also reveal our hidden weaknesses and hidden strengths, opening us up to the fragility of life and to the kindness of strangers.

This retreat is the perfect opportunity to spend some time in the presence of a loving God who is waiting to welcome us, nurture us, and draw us into deeper relationship. The Incarnation shows how it was vital to God's plan for him to draw near to us in the flesh as God-with-us. The retreat allows us to meditate on the ways in which God chooses this way to make his love known and to give us strength in the Word made flesh.

ADVENT RETREAT: SESSION 1
God with Us

Invitation to Stillness

We usually prepare for an important meeting or conversation by focusing our mind and body so that we can be fully present. At the beginning of each session we will suggest a stillness exercise and lead you through it. We begin today by inviting you to notice your breathing, the rhythm of it, and the feel and sound of each breath as you inhale and exhale. With each in-breath, allow yourself to focus on the here and now. With each out-breath, let go of any tension or concern you may feel other than being here, still, in this space. John's Gospel tells us that God is with us. God is here now, waiting to fill you with grace and peace.

Reading

John 1–6, 9–12, 14.

In the beginning was the Word, and the Word was with God, and the Word was God. He was in the beginning with God. All things came into being through him, and without him not one thing came into being. What has come into being in him was life, and the life was the light of all people. The light shines in the darkness, and the darkness did not overcome it. . . .

The true light, which enlightens everyone, was coming into the world. He was in the world, and the world came into being through him; yet the world did not know him. He came to what was his own, and his own people did not accept him. But to all who received him, who believed in his name, he gave power to become children of God. . . .

And the Word became flesh and lived among us, and we have seen his glory, the glory as of a Father's only son, full of grace and truth.

Reflect

- John tells us that, from the very beginning, God's deepest nature and identity is to be Word, life and light. This is who God is, and God wants to share that nature and identity with us. God wants to speak, to be in relationship with us. God wants to breathe life into us and into the whole of creation. God is in my life and God *is* my life. There is no darkness in God. Nothing in my life or in the world can ever be stronger than God's love, shining through Jesus. Anyone who accepts the Word made flesh receives power to become the child of a God who is patient and gracious, waiting for us to accept the gift of grace and truth, offered freely and without condition.

• The prologue to John's Gospel tells us that we have a choice: to accept the Word made flesh or not. All the stories we hear during Advent show God offering the gift of his presence. Mary and Joseph, Zechariah and Elizabeth, wise men and shepherds, kings and inn-keepers, all receive the same offer. In the face of the unfamiliar we can open ourselves to the God of surprises and embrace it as a gift, or we can fall silent and reject the opportunity as a threat. The choice is ours.

Talk to God

• How do I feel as I hear the gospel speak of God's plan to share our human life from the inside? How do I react to the thought of God's light shining in the darkness? Perhaps I've been feeling 'in the dark' this year. This retreat is an opportunity to share with God how that darkness has felt for me. Has anything 'come to light' that I hadn't noticed before: about me, about my life and relationships, about the world around me? I take some time to savour the words: 'light shines in darkness, and darkness could not overpower it.'

- I listen again to these words: 'He was in the world that had come into being through him, and the world did not recognise him. He came to his own and his own people did not accept him.' What has helped me recently to recognise and accept God, present to me in my daily life? In times of trouble it can be hard to believe that God is truly with us, that we are in God's hands, come what may. Have the difficulties of this year challenged my capacity to live in faith, hope and love? Or have I found them growing in me, despite it all?

- John tells us that 'to those who did accept him he gave power to become children of God.' What does it mean to me to be given that power? I turn my thoughts to the many people on whom I depend: my family and friends, service workers who make my life possible, anyone I have encountered as a strength, and I support those who have turned to me for support. What does it mean for me to see them as God's children, my brothers and sisters?

- I ask God to shine the light of grace and truth into my heart, so that I can see myself and the world around me with his merciful eyes. As I enter into Advent, I name the graces that I need and desire at this time. I spend some time quietly allowing God's word to take root and become flesh in me.

ADVENT RETREAT: SESSION 2
How Can This Be?

Invitation to Stillness

As you begin this time of prayer, allow your body to settle into a peaceful and comfortable position. Let your mind settle, putting your preoccupations into God's hands for this time. Listen to the sounds around you, focusing in from those far away to those nearest to you: the sounds within your room, the sound of your own breathing, relaxing as you hear each breath drawn.

Mary listened to God's word and pondered it in her heart. Open your heart and mind to what God is trying to announce to you right now.

Reading

Luke 1:26–38

In the sixth month the angel Gabriel was sent by God to a town in Galilee called Nazareth, to a virgin engaged to a man whose name was Joseph, of the house of David. The virgin's name was Mary. And he came to her and said, 'Greetings, favoured one! The Lord is with you.' But she was much perplexed by his words and pondered what sort of greeting this might be. The angel said to her, 'Do not be afraid, Mary, for you have found favour with God. And now, you will conceive in your womb and bear a son, and you will name him Jesus. He will be great, and will be called the Son of the Most High, and the Lord God will give to him the throne of his ancestor David. He will reign over the house of Jacob for ever, and of his kingdom there will be no end.' Mary said to the angel, 'How can this be, since I am a virgin?' The angel said to her, 'The Holy Spirit will come upon you, and the power of the Most High will overshadow you; therefore the child to be born will be holy; he will be called Son of God. And now, your relative Elizabeth in her old age has also conceived a son; and this is the sixth month for her who was said to be barren. For nothing will be impossible with God.' Then Mary said, 'Here am I, the servant of the Lord; let it be with me according to your word.' Then the angel departed from her.

Reflect

- It's not easy to imagine the Annunciation. We don't know for certain what happened or how Mary experienced God's extraordinary communication. Medieval paintings are beautiful but often depict an exalted event, far from the mess and chaos of human reality. If Mary was at home the domestic setting would be simple and cluttered, full of the banal, everyday features of a girl's life in a humble environment. Perhaps she saw the solid figure of an angel, or perhaps this happened in a dream. Perhaps it began as an inner whisper that gathered and grew into something clear and unmistakable. What we do know is that Mary's first reaction was to ask questions: How can this be? Why me? How can I be sure? How will I manage? These are questions many of us have grappled with at crossroad moments in our lives.

- As a woman Mary has little or no value in her society except in relation to someone else. Yet on her response hangs the fate of the whole human race. She feels uncertain, inadequate to the task, confused. But she also has faith in God, and has a generous heart, and is willing to take risks and go forward, trusting that God will be with her.

- In Mary, God-with-us will come to life in her if only she will allow this to happen. God knows her fears and waits patiently for her to make the choice. God knows what is in our deepest heart— better than we know it ourselves. God's way of dealing with us is through collaboration, not dictatorship. Knowing our hesitations, doubts and fears, God waits in both the crucial and the trivial moments of our lives for us to say yes.

Talk to God

- Has there been a sense for me, this year, of something wanting to come to birth? This has been an uncertain time, with many unusual demands on us as we adjust to a 'new normal'. Perhaps there has been a sense of loss, of the death of what felt safe and familiar. Have I been able to share this with God, allowing myself the vulnerability of mourning, or have I turned in on myself, relying on my own resources?

- If there has been loss and threat, perhaps there has also been a sense of opportunity, of new pathways opening up. What strengths and graces have I needed in order to respond to the world as it is now? I ask God to widen my horizons, to give me the strength of mind and heart to see where this new way of being me in the world may lead.

- The word 'angel' means messenger. What messages from God am I hearing right now? What kind of messenger am I able to be to those around me? I can be good news or bad news—the choice is mine. I spend some time with God, listening as deeply as I can to what God is announcing to me.

ADVENT RETREAT: SESSION 3
Do Not Be Afraid

Invitation to Stillness

As you come into God's presence, know that God is already here, waiting for you. Allow yourself to let go of any tension you may be carrying in your body, allowing the muscles to relax from your head, neck and face, all down your spine and lower body to your feet. Let the stillness take over and lead you to a space where you can make room for the God of dreams to be with you.

Reading

Joel 2:21–29

> Do not fear, O soil; be glad and rejoice, for the LORD has done great things!
> Do not fear, you animals of the field, for the pastures of the wilderness are green;
> the tree bears its fruit, the fig tree and vine give their full yield.
>
> O children of Zion, be glad and rejoice in the LORD your God;
> for he has given the early rain for your vindication,

he has poured down for you abundant rain, the
    early and the later rain, as before.
The threshing-floors shall be full of grain, the
    vats shall overflow with wine and oil.

I will repay you for the years that the swarming
    locust has eaten,
the hopper, the destroyer, and the cutter, my
    great army, which I sent against you.

You shall eat in plenty and be satisfied, and
    praise the name of the LORD your God,
who has dealt wondrously with you. And my
    people shall never again be put to shame.
You shall know that I am in the midst of Israel,
    and that I, the LORD, am your God and there
    is no other.
And my people shall never again be put to
    shame.

Then afterward I will pour out my spirit on all
    flesh; your sons and your daughters shall
    prophesy,
your old men shall dream dreams, and your
    young men shall see visions.
Even on the male and female slaves, in those
    days, I will pour out my spirit.

Reflect

- The Joseph of the Old Testament, Joseph with the coat of many colours, was called the Dreamer by his brothers, and they didn't mean it kindly! They didn't need people of vision—they needed people who could be realistic about the problems facing them . . . Joseph the carpenter of Nazareth is also portrayed as a man of dreams, but his dreams are nightmares. Mary, the love of his life, appears to have shamed and betrayed him. His dreams of love, marriage, a home and family are shattered. But in his dream he is told by the angel, 'Don't be afraid.' The same greeting as for Mary, the same invitation to a leap of faith, hope and love.

- In Joel's prophecy, old men dream dreams and young men see visions. Medieval art often portrays Joseph as an old man, beyond the longings of romantic love, but we don't know how old he actually was. If he was a young man he would have had hopes of fruitfulness—the 'quiver full' of children promised as a blessing in the Psalms—but now he feels cheated, empty and barren, without hope for the future.

- But the prophecy promises overflowing fruitfulness as God's Spirit overshadows the whole earth—not just the insiders, those who belong to the Covenant, but also outsiders and rejects, the slaves on the margins of society. God's Spirit doesn't bring only human beings to life but also the soil and the animals—everything is brought to fulfilment in this great promise of the Day of the Lord. The angel reassures Joseph: it's good to be a dreamer; take Mary as your wife and follow your heart, for the dream you share is God's dream for the whole of creation, made flesh in the Incarnation.

Talk to God

- I let the words of Joel's prophecy sink into my heart and mind. Perhaps one phrase or word has particularly struck me and I take time to savour it, allowing God to touch my heart. Advent is a time for reflecting on God's promised gifts of grace and truth. What graces do I want to ask for right now? What truth do I want to understand and live more deeply?

- Perhaps I've had disappointments, like Joseph. The disappointed disciples on the road to Emmaus had lost hope, saying to Jesus, 'we had hoped . . . '. Can I share with God any hopes or dreams that have been frustrated, and what that feels like?

- God also invites us in this Advent time to enter deeply into his dream for the whole of creation. Pope Francis speaks of God calling us to live together as sisters and brothers, filling the earth and making known the values of goodness, love and peace. All creation will enjoy the fruits of this promise, which appears in the prologue of John's Gospel—those who accept Jesus into their lives will become children of God. How does it feel to be filled with the hope of that promise?

- I take time to talk to God about any disappointments or hopes that come to mind, and put all my dreams for the world into the hands of our loving Creator.

ADVENT RETREAT: SESSION 4
Going Home by Another Way

Invitation to Stillness

As you come into this time of prayer, allow your senses to lead you into stillness. What can you hear beyond the music? Can you hear the sounds outside and inside where you are? Perhaps there is a scent from a candle, the freshness of the cool air, or of rain, or you feel warmth against the cold outside. Let your senses draw you into the present moment and the presence of our Creator.

Reading

Matthew 2:9–12

When they had heard the king, they set out; and there, ahead of them, went the star that they had seen at its rising, until it stopped over the place where the child was. When they saw that the star had stopped, they were overwhelmed with joy. On entering the house, they saw the child with Mary his mother; and they knelt down and paid him homage. Then, opening their treasure-chests, they offered him gifts of gold, frankincense and myrrh. And having been warned in a dream not to return to Herod, they left for their own country by another road.

Reflect

- We talk of 'seeing stars' when we've had a knock on the head that makes us dizzy. That kind of experience leaves us feeling out of kilter, knocked off our balance. Perhaps this is how the wise men felt. They were used to consulting the stars as a source of wisdom and guidance that operated by well-known rules. Yet, suddenly, here is a star that doesn't behave in the normal way, and here is an experience that confounds all their expectations.

- The mysterious, all-powerful God is born in poverty, far from royal palaces and the corridors

of power. The wise men bring with them treasures, symbols of the power of wealth and status,
knowledge and wisdom, life and death. Yet they
lay them at the feet of a newborn baby born of a
humble mother and watched over by a carpenter
and some wandering shepherds. Nothing they see
is as was predicted.

• What they meet in Bethlehem is the God of surprises, the wild and unpredictable God who can
never be tamed or domesticated. This is God who
calls us to go home 'by another way'. Maybe we've
got used to the well-worn path. Not everyone
likes surprises, and we may have let ourselves get
comfortable and complacent, hanging on to our
safety belts. And here is God calling us out of
ourselves—step out of your comfort zone, take a
walk on the wild side. . . .

• As he grew older Jesus called many people to step
off the familiar path. He called Samaritans and
Jews, priests and prostitutes, Levites and lepers to
become members of one family, united in love and
service of one another. This is what it means to
accept him into our lives and become children of
God. We come home to God by God's path, not
our own. We make the path by walking in faith
and trust, with open minds and hearts.

Talk to God

- What is the star by which I have navigated my life's journey? What are the things that I have relied on to help me feel safe and secure, well settled in my own place? Perhaps this year has made me hold on even tighter to my securities. But perhaps there has been another call, a still, small voice inviting me to live other choices and different relationships. Can I listen to that voice now, in the silence?

- What are the treasures of my life? Jesus says, 'Where your treasure is, there will your heart be also.' What gives me a sense of power and status? What makes me feel fragile and vulnerable? As I take time to be still, can I share with God my desires and anxieties, my dreads and my dreams? Do I have a sense of God offering me gifts right now?

- I sit quietly with Jesus, who is sleeping in his mother's arms. What do I want to say to him? To her? Perhaps I want to hold him, the child of promise, my guiding star. Or perhaps I don't feel worthy to touch him. Can I allow God, the Word made Flesh, to touch me?

ADVENT RETREAT: SESSION 5
A Future Full of Hope

Invitation to Stillness

I come to this time of quiet prayer with a desire to be still, to be present to God. Perhaps my mind is racing. Perhaps, when life is so busy, this feels like wasted time. But I offer God the gift of this time and allow the minutes to flow by, without measuring or counting. Breathing in and out, I allow myself to rest in the moment.

Reading

Matthew 2:13–21

Now after [the wise men] had left, an angel of the Lord appeared to Joseph in a dream and said, 'Get up, take the child and his mother, and flee to Egypt, and remain there until I tell you; for Herod is about to search for the child, to destroy him.' Then Joseph got up, took the child and his mother by night, and went to Egypt and remained there until the death of Herod . . .

When Herod saw that he had been tricked by the wise men, he was infuriated, and he sent and killed all the children in and around Bethlehem who were two years old or under, according to the time that he had learned from the wise men. Then was fulfilled what had been spoken through the prophet Jeremiah:

'A voice was heard in Ramah, wailing and loud lamentation,
Rachel weeping for her children; she refused to be consoled, because they are no more.'

When Herod died, an angel of the Lord suddenly appeared in a dream to Joseph in Egypt and said, 'Get up, take the child and his mother, and go to the land of Israel, for those who were seeking the child's life are dead.' Then Joseph got up, took the child and his mother, and went to the land of Israel.

Reflect

- This is hardly a happy Christmas scene: refugees fleeing amid terror and destruction, children murdered by an oppressive ruler, homelessness and desolate mourning. Matthew's Gospel tells of Rachel weeping for her children and refusing to be comforted. But this quotation from Jeremiah is a prophecy full of joy, hope and consolation. God says: 'Keep your voice from weeping, and your eyes from tears, for there is a reward for your work . . . there is hope for your future' (Jeremiah 31:16–17).

- Every day our newspapers are full of violence and destruction, cruelty and death, racism and oppression of many kinds. It would be easy to despair, especially as we face an uncertain future. But in the midst of all this, God is with us, offering us a future full of hope. We ourselves can be part of that hope for the future of the world.

- If we allow ourselves to be led by the way of Jesus, sharing the faith and courage of Joseph and Mary, the trust of the shepherds and wise men, the welcome of Elizabeth and all the familiar figures of the Nativity, we will find ourselves making real the story of Christ's birth. This is the true Christmas present—God's gift to us, but also our gift to God.

- Christmas songs and carols sing of us wanting to bring a gift to Jesus in the manger. What can we bring but our willingness to have our hearts transformed by the wonderful generosity of God? God wants nothing more from us than that willingness, so that his dream of being with us can be fulfilled.

Talk to God

- The Christmas story is full of journeys, both physical and spiritual. No one involved in the story of the Incarnation is left in the same place that they started from. God's invitation waits for our response, but never leaves us standing. I may find myself shying away from the harder parts of the story—this is not the safe and happy Christmas of childhood. How do I react to the harsher parts of the narrative, where nothing feels safe or stable? I take time to get into the minds of Joseph and Mary as they pack up and escape, with horror following close behind them. Perhaps I talk to them or share in their conversation with each other. What does it feel like, to try and keep faith and hope alive in such a situation? What do I find myself wanting to say to God?

- Jesus is so small and vulnerable. He escapes, while others die. I allow my thoughts to dwell on the many refugees and terrified children, the desperate families on our own borders right now, trying to find shelter and a new life. Have these Advent meditations changed the way I think of them? How do I see God-with-us in them?

- Finally, I sit quietly and allow God to speak to me through the Scriptures. Perhaps I can take time to find Jeremiah's prophecy and share in Rachel's joy, despite her weeping and desolation. How do these Scripture passages speak to me in times of joy or of sadness? Are there joys and sorrows I want to share with God right now? Joseph is presented as a model of obedience, a word that means to listen attentively. How am I being called in my own life to listen attentively to God's promises?

Conclusion

As our Advent Retreat ends, it may be helpful to spend some time reflecting on the process as a whole. Has this time of prayerful pondering on God's word moved your heart in any way or led you to think differently about the entry into human life of God-with-us? Is there a Scripture passage or word that has become special to you? In what way have you encountered God-with-you in the events of your life or in the world around you?

There are many practical as well as spiritual implications to the Christmas story. Did you find yourself struggling at any point, or resisting the words and meaning of the Scriptures you read? You may find it helpful to look back at any insights you received or any sense of invitation to respond to God's word. Has anything emerged that needs healing or transformation? Has there been a sense of growth in courage to move something forward or forge a new path? Where might God be leading you home 'by another way'?

The Christmas story is one of surprises, and of people allowing God into their lives in unexpected ways. Above all it's a story of obedience, of people listening attentively to God's dream and sharing it in their own way, each according to their capacity. Take some time to explore any sense you have had of grace being offered, to ask for the courage to respond, and to thank God for every gift: those recognised and acted upon, and those yet to be understood and realised. Perhaps you can offer God the Christmas gift of your time and attention in the days to come as you continue on the road to Bethlehem with Jesus Emmanuel, God-with-us.

O Wisdom . . . Lord and ruler . . . Root of Jesse . . . Key of David . . . Rising Sun . . . King of the Nations . . . Emmanuel . . . Come, Lord Jesus.

CHRISTMAS

Christmas

Introduction to Christmas

The birth of any child is always a source of wonder, when we feel closer to the mystery of life and, in a most natural way, the mystery of God is brought near. In the birth of Jesus, we see our God made visible and so are caught up in love of the God we cannot see. The thrilling reality of the Word made flesh is both gift and call. In the words of the first letter of John, 'Beloved, since God loved us so much, we also ought to love one another' (1 John 4:11). We are challenged to love the God we cannot see in the neighbour we can see. There can be no separation of these two realities: to love God is to love your neighbour and to love your neighbour is to love God.

Prayer

Today love itself became flesh like one of us, so that you, O God, might see and love in us what you see and love in him. May we see you and love you in our brothers and sisters. Through Christ our Lord. Amen.

Kieran O'Mahony OSA,
with prayers by John Byrne OSA,
Hearers of the Word: Praying & Exploring the Readings
Advent & Christmas: Year C

Christmas Reflections

Christmas Eve

Fr John Casey was a priest in my home parish. He was a curate in Cloonloo (County Sligo) and I never met him. He died nearly a quarter of a century before I was born. I grew up feeling I knew him though, and he has been part of my life—as sure and certain as any person I number among my friends and family. He mattered to me and still does. That's why I want to bring him to the pages of these reflections. I think he has a story to tell.

My mother spoke often of Fr Casey. She concluded every prayer we said as a family, or maybe just the two of us in a car, with the words 'an Our Father and three Hail Marys to ask Fr Casey to ask God to help us and keep us free from accidents and harm at home and on the road'. This was her 'optional extra' to any prayer she said. Fr Casey mattered to her and it seemed important that his memory would matter to us as well.

She told me once that on Christmas Day (1930) Fr Casey walked into her home with Christmas gifts for her two younger brothers and herself. It was the first Christmas after their father had died, and he wanted to bring a little kindness to their home. She even remembered the toy he had bought for her—a small red car. This act of kindness seems to have been at the heart of my mother's absolute wish to keep Fr Casey's memory alive and fresh for all of us. It wasn't until my mother died a few years ago that I made the connection with the full significance of this story.

She was born in 1923 so her father died when she was about seven years of age, and she was the oldest. It became clear to me then why a priest, an obviously good and holy priest, would want to do the right thing by a young family facing into Christmas Day without their father.

Fr Casey died in 1939 and my mother some seventy years later. She never allowed his story or the place he held in her memory to be lost or forgotten. There's a question here I believe: in seventy years' time, for what will *we* be remembered?

As we face into Christmas Eve now—the shopping is done, the food has been ordered, the travel plans have been made and the decorations and tree are in place and working—concentrate now on the story 'this is how Jesus Christ came to be born' (Matthew 1:18–25). Make it your own, take it to your heart and remember that Christ comes to you this Christmas to bring joy and peace to you and yours, to your home and parish and to our country and world. Tell this story, retell it so that generations to come may come to know it as theirs too.

Vincent Sherlock,
Let Advent Be Advent

Christmas Day

Christmas can be like a magnifying glass. When life is good, then things are great, and when things are not so good, then life can take on awful proportions. It is as if the situations of life are magnified at Christmas due to the level of expectation we have around the feast.

Of course it'd be wonderful for everyone to have a peaceful, fun-filled celebration, but if that were to happen some of us would have to be very good actors. We can't avoid what's real. One Christmas morning I went out to celebrate Mass. It was a small church, and with a quick scan I absorbed who was and wasn't there that morning. I had my homily ready, but I had to rethink it immediately.

On my right, as I looked down from the altar, sat a young couple with the cutest newborn baby in their arms. Both parents were besotted and proud. They were delighted with the number of people who came up to congratulate them, and they indulged themselves in the good wishes of so many. On my left sat a couple who only three days beforehand had gone through the pain of the loss of their baby as a result of a miscarriage. They were a little older than most couples and not only were they ravaged by the loss, but they wondered if they could ever, ever conceive and have a child again. One couple looked out to seek the congratulations of the assembled, the other looked down, afraid that others would see the pain and sadness which they couldn't hide. It would have been easier not to come to church that Christmas morning.

I don't know what I said that morning, but it didn't refer to either situation as I couldn't ignore the joy of one and the torment of the other. When it came to the sign of peace, I paused for a moment and said, 'You know we often use the sign of peace to say hello to someone or share a comment or two.' There were a lot of people in the church at that stage, and it was slightly uncomfortable as the air was humid. I continued, 'Sometimes I feel like a hypocrite offering the sign of peace because there is someone in the church that I don't get on with, and yes there may even be someone I can't stand but such is life. . . . I am not as Christian as I'd like to be.' Another pause from me. 'I often see the sign of peace, especially at Christmas, not as an offering of peace but a hope that peace is possible where there presently may be little or no peace. . . . Let us offer one another a sign of Christ's peace.' I noticed the couple on my left hug for quite a few moments, and I made sure to offer them my peace; both clasped my hand tightly. About sixteen months later I baptised their newborn child.

This year, no matter what the magnifying glass throws up, please pray for the peace that is possible for you or for someone else—'The Peace of Christ be with you.'

Alan Hilliard,
Dipping into Advent

Mary, the Mother of God

Luke's Gospel portrays Mary as saying 'yes' to God's call to her to become the mother of God's Son. Yet the gospel suggests that her response to God's call did not come easily to her. Initially she was 'deeply disturbed' by the greeting of the angel. She raised a probing question in response to the further words of the angel. 'How can this come about?' she asked. She eventually arrived at the point where she could say, 'Let what you have said be done to me.' However, the reading suggests that she only came to that point after a lot of struggle. We are reminded of Jesus in the garden of Gethsemane. His prayer eventually brought him to the point where he could say, 'not my will but yours be done'. Again, that was only after a great struggle, in the course of which he had prayed, 'remove this cup from me'.

The experiences of Mary and of Jesus suggest that responding to God's call, remaining faithful to God's will for our lives, always involve a struggle of some kind. The nature of that struggle will be different for each of us. However, we engage in that struggle knowing that we are not alone in it. The power of the Most High will overshadow us, as it overshadowed Mary; the Holy Spirit will come upon us, as it came upon Mary. In our struggle to be faithful, we are also encouraged by the words of Gabriel to Mary: 'nothing is impossible to God'. As Mary's adult son, Jesus, will go on to say, 'for God all things are possible'. Mary herself is also a resource in our struggle to be faithful to the Lord's call, which is why we ask her to intercede for us, to 'pray for us sinners, now and at the hour of our death'.

Martin Hogan,
The Word Is Near You, on Your Lips and in Your Heart

The Holy Family

We often remember the sacrifices our parents made for us. Financial generosity, giving their time, understanding us when we go wrong. The first family story of Jesus is a tough story—Joseph caring for him and Mary through the dangers of the journey into Egypt and back, like asylum seekers or refugees today fleeing from danger in their country.

We salute the love of parents, siblings, guardians, grandparents and extended families; we remember at different times of life how much they did for us and gave to us.

In the difficulties of family life today, the role of the Church is to support family life of all kinds with education, faith formation, political structures that support family life, being there for families in bad times like illness and death, and providing a place to celebrate family life in marriage and baptism. Parishes try to be committed to supporting family life.

Jesus came not only to be with us, but to care. This is the call to the Church: to be in the world and to be for the world.

'Joseph took the child and his mother.' He was a caring man, looking after them, making a huge difference to a small number of people—this is the message of love in the Gospel and is the central message of the feast today.

Donal Neary SJ,
Gospel Reflections for Sundays of Year A

The Epiphany

The word 'Epiphany' means a showing forth, a setting in the light. Today we celebrate the good news
that God showed forth his Son to all the nations,
Jews and pagans alike. It is the pagan visitors from
the unnamed city of the east who reveal to us how
to respond to God's showing forth of his Son, God's
gift of his Son. Jesus was born into a Jewish world
and these visitors from the east were strangers in that
world; they were outsiders. It often takes strangers,
outsiders, to show us how to respond to God's gift
of his Son, how to appreciate the great riches of our
faith, the presence of Christ in the Eucharist and in
the other sacraments, and the life-giving message of
the Scriptures, in particular, the Gospels. In recent
years there has been a huge increase in the number of
people coming to live among us from abroad, many of
them from the east, from Eastern Europe, and from
much further east, the Far East, others from the south,
and from Africa. They often bring an enthusiasm and
appreciation for the treasures of the faith that we,
perhaps, have lost somewhat. They have enriched the
Church by their readiness to share their gifts and ener-
gies with the Church here in their adopted homeland.

Although in the emerging tradition of the Church
the visitors from the east have become kings and are
portrayed as kings in our traditional cribs, they are
not called kings in the Gospels. They are called 'magi',

translated as 'wise men'. The term 'magi' referred to people who had special knowledge, experts in some field or other, and in the case of our magi, it would appear, experts in astronomy or astrology. The rising of a new star suggested to these 'magi' the birth of a new Jewish king, to whom they wished to do homage. They saw a new light and they chose to follow the light, wherever it led them. They represent all those, of whatever creed or persuasion, who seek to follow the light, the light of truth. The magi are the ancestors of all of us who seek the truth. It was their own natural skills of searching and interpreting the skies—their own natural knowledge and wisdom—that launched them on their search. Those natural gifts brought them to Jerusalem, but the Gospel reading suggests that they needed the guidance of the Jewish Scriptures to direct them to Bethlehem, where the infant king of the Jews would be found. Reason and the revelation of Scripture worked together to bring them to the Lord. Their profile in the Gospels reminds us that our natural gifts of mind and reason need never be an obstacle to faith. The magi came to recognise that the brightest star of all was Christ the Lord; he was 'light from light', in the words of the Creed.

Martin Hogan,
*The Word Is Near You, on Your Lips
and in Your Heart*

ORDINARY TIME

Ordinary Time

Introduction to Ordinary Time

When people hear the word 'ordinary' they immediately think of something plain, unremarkable, the opposite of extraordinary. We often tend to think of Ordinary Time as a sort of 'everything else' season—if it's not Advent, Christmas, Lent or Easter, it is Ordinary Time. Yet we should not dismiss this season or treat it as an anti-climax or downtime in between the big feasts. The term itself comes from the Latin *ordinalis*, meaning ordered, so it simply refers to the way the Sundays are named in a numbered sequence. The rhythm of the liturgical seasons also reflects the cycle of life in the natural world and the rhythm of our own lives.

During Ordinary Time we hear the stories of Jesus' life and ministry through his teaching and parables, through his meals and healings, through his conversations with followers and challengers, right up to his final journey towards and into Jerusalem. In following them we get a real sense of journeying with Jesus and of his vision of the kingdom of heaven as a way of life in the here and now.

There is much richness to be discovered when we allow the story to unfold from one Sunday to the next. We are invited to be active participants in the gospel story, using it as a time to draw closer to Jesus and to grow and mature in our understanding and faith. Don't let this anything-but-ordinary time pass you by.

While defined as one season in the Church calendar, Ordinary Time is broken into two different periods. The first of these runs from the Baptism of the Lord to the start of Lent, and the second from just after Pentecost right up to the first Sunday of Advent, when the new liturgical year starts again.

The Season of Creation

The Season of Creation is a relatively new season in the Catholic Liturgical calendar but one that has been celebrated across many Christian churches for the past twenty-five years. As most of us are aware, we are living through a devastating environmental crisis, where the very fabric of the ecosystems of our planet is unravelling. Seventy per cent of wildlife has been destroyed in the past forty years due to human activity. The continuing rise in toxic greenhouse gas emissions is fueling a climate crisis that is making parts of our world uninhabitable for human beings. It is the world's poorest who are suffering the most now, and it will be even worse for future generations. What is most disturbing is that the scientists are sounding the alarm bells loud and clear, yet the world is not responding with the urgency that is needed. Pope Francis describes the roots of the environmental crisis as deeply spiritual, therefore faith communities have a clear role to play in inspiring an ecological conversion amongst believers.

And so, within Ordinary Time, the Season of Creation gives us an opportunity to come together to renew our relationship with God's creation. It runs from the World Day of Prayer for Creation on 1 September to the Feast of St Francis of Assisi on 4 October. It has its origins in the Orthodox Church, which in 1989 proclaimed 1 September as a day of prayer for creation. Subsequently, the World Council of Churches extended the celebration until 4 October. Many Christians around the world embraced this idea, and in 2015 Pope Francis officially declared 1 September the World Day of Prayer for Creation in the Catholic calendar. This means that the world's 2.2 billion Christians now celebrate the Season of Creation as an ecumenical occasion worldwide.

Tríona Doherty and Jane Mellet,
*The Deep End: A Journey with the Sunday Gospels
in the Year of Matthew*

Ordinary Time Reflections

Love That Pours Itself Out

Lord, it is good to chat, and I find myself looking forward to meeting you. Let me start by telling you my best thinking about you. I know the beautiful statement of St John, that 'God is love' (John 3:16). But your love can't be thought of as static. It is always being poured out, inexhaustibly and richly. You yourself use the term 'poured out' at the Last Supper, I notice. Often the Holy Spirit is described as being 'poured out' on everyone.

Perhaps it is your very nature to be poured out, and this is at the heart of the universe? I have an image of this love as a great waterfall: am I being invited to come ever closer to it and to be drenched by its spray? Is this the deepest meaning of my life, whether I know it or not? Am I being constantly called into an unfathomable depth of loving relationships, since you, who are three divine persons, endlessly pour out your love on each other and on me too? Could it be that I, like a child, am being invited to 'dance' with you? Perhaps you are untiringly calling to me, 'we'd like you to make a fourth!'

Some writers speak about the endless laughter of the divine persons. One author says, 'In the core of the Trinity the Father laughs and gives birth to the Son. The Son laughs back at the Father and gives birth to the Spirit. The whole Trinity laughs and gives birth to you!' It does me good, Lord, to feel that I share in the laughter that rings across the universe. You yourself have said, 'blessed are you who weep, because you shall laugh'. Don't let me confuse divine intimacy with solemnity: you are a laughing as well as a loving God! You are indeed love that pours itself out.

Brian Grogan SJ,
I Am Infinitely Loved

St Brigid

The tradition about Brigid that has come down to us speaks of a woman who had a great love of God and who gave her life to God in the face of family opposition. She knew herself to be a friend of God. Because she experienced God's friendship in her own life, she was able to reveal God's friendship to others. She was especially good and kind to the poor and those in greatest need. She knew that God had a special love for them. Brigid often gave away food to those who were poor and hungry. She welcomed all who visited her. She lived the kind of life that Jesus speaks about in the Gospel reading when he called on us to be loving and forgiving and to give generously to others. She lived like Jesus. People soon realised that Brigid was a very special person who had a deep relationship with the Lord and she gathered a community around her. We can pray to St Brigid in heaven. We can ask her to help us to live like Jesus as she did, to be as loving and kind as she was. Brigid gave new life to people by her kindness and generosity. February 1 is not only the feast of St Brigid, it is also Imbolc, an ancient Celtic festival that marks the start of spring. We speak of Brigid as one who welcomes the spring. She is the saint of springtime.

Brigid not only took special care of people, she was also remembered as one who cared for animals and nature. She teaches us to care for all of God's creation. St Brigid's cross is her traditional symbol. It speaks to us of nature, as it is made from rushes or straw. People often place it in their homes, perhaps over the door or in the window, because they believe it brings a very special blessing to the house and to all who live there. On her feast, we ask St Brigid to bless each one of us by helping us to be as generous and loving as she was towards all in need, and as respectful as she was towards our natural environment.

Martin Hogan,
*The Word Is Near You, on Your Lips
and in Your Heart*

Enough

Being grateful for the moment while it's here, that's what matters. Being grateful for what it is in itself, not hankering for something that may come next—something that may be starting to take shape in our busy and ambitious minds.

Recently an American writer and some old college friends were having their annual get together, catching up on how life was treating them. They also exchanged news, of course, about absent friends. One of those friends had been flying very high indeed. He was a banker on Wall Street and they reckoned he was now earning more in a day than any of the rest of them would earn, if they were lucky, in a month.

'And yet,' said the writer, 'I have something that he will never have.' 'What's that?' he was asked.

'Enough.'

The word intrigues me. We know that there are millions of people in our world who quite obviously don't have 'enough'. They suffer from lack of food, housing, medical care. But we can assume that the Wall Street millionaire has had no personal experience of such deprivation—nor probably have any of the people talking about him.

What the writer is saying is that becoming rich has compelled the man on Wall Street to become richer, and that becoming richer will compel him to become richer still. Now there's a sense in which that doesn't make him all that different from many of the rest of us. Ambition, the urge to do better, to aim for higher goals, is part of our make-up as human beings. It's a common characteristic which hasn't just created individual fortunes, it has made possible all kinds of advances in society.

However, in personal terms, a drive towards getting more and always more is a drive that can never be satisfied. The driven person will never be able to say, 'This is enough.' When the writer says that he himself has enough, I don't think he's just talking about money. I think he's echoing a line from the poet R. S. Thomas, 'life is not hurrying on to a receding future'. Now and then, we need to stop hurrying. We need to become aware of ourselves as we are.

There's a hill-top above Rostrevor where I often like to sit, usually in silence, looking down across a forest to the waters of Carlingford Lough. I think of nothing much beyond the peace of being there. In such moments I can say yes, I have enough.

Denis Tuohy,
Streets and Sacred Places:
Reflections of a News Reporter

Feast of the Assumption
Mary always remained a child, totally dependent upon God, gladly receiving everything from God's hands, and never wanting to be apart from him. Mary's spirit is the spirit of childhood, a combination of utter powerlessness and immense confidence. A child is small and helpless, yet isn't closed in on itself but delights in the world around it, full of a sense of wonder and trust. A child walks along the road of life with a spirit of astonishment, and with enough confidence to believe that God may appear at any turn. Mary looked at the path of life with the eyes of a child.

We could all gain a lot by recovering this spirit of childhood, by becoming again faithful to the children we once were. One of Pope Francis's favourite poems puts this well. It is by Friedrich Hölderlin, and is dedicated to his grandmother. It finishes with the line; 'May the man hold fast to what the child has promised.' The child is filled with hope because it sees beauty everywhere, a beauty that is invisible to sceptics and cynics. Mary had that childlike spirit, that transparency and that simplicity, because she surrendered herself completely to God.

Thomas Casey SJ,
Smile of Joy: Mary of Nazareth

Season of Creation

We talk easily about what's happening on the surface of our lives. But what's really going on? Beneath the surface level of life on earth lies a strategy, backed by divine power and artistry, that is sweeping everything up into one infinitely complex whole, so that finally God may become all in all. Even to glimpse occasionally that this is what's really going on gives hope, and is an antidote to the view that our common home can never be put to rights, and that human history will end in tragic burnout. We are to live and work in hope, 'with the eyes of our hearts enlightened'. This is what mysticism is about.

The insights of science about the cosmos are coming to us thick and fast. Our generation is being showered with insights about the history and structure of creation which were hidden from our predecessors. This new knowledge helps us to understand God's artistic work, appreciate it properly and relate lovingly to its creator. Creation is God's self-revelation, and we have so much to learn from it. Then we can participate more effectively in co-creating and restoring the divine masterpiece.

Brian Grogan SJ,
*Finding God in a Leaf:
The Mysticism of* Laudato Sí

God with Us

We hear Jesus himself saying, 'I am not alone. He who sent me is with me' (John 16:32). This simple phrase 'with me' is enough to indicate all that is going on: Jesus has been commissioned by his Father for a particular task, but he can feel inadequate for it, as the agony in Gethsemane makes clear (Mark 14:32–36). Nonetheless, as John tells us, God will be 'with' him to support him, as the angel did in Gethsemane (Luke 22:43), and his Father will not forsake him in spite of his feeling of dereliction (Matthew 27:46).

We should keep an eye and an ear open in the liturgy and in our reading of the Bible to pick up the many references to God being 'with' us and his other chosen servants, so that we can appreciate their full theological significance. This should encourage us to appreciate the depth and all the implications of the apparently simple universal greeting with which we Christians are so familiar that it glides off our minds regularly without our appreciating it: 'The Lord be with you.' Hearing this from the priest at Mass should stop us regularly in our tracks: it is not just a blessing; it is always also a challenge. As we see throughout the Bible, it implies a previous particular commission that we have personally received from God. It should remind us that God promises to be always 'with' us, as the risen Jesus promised his disciples (Matthew 28:20), regardless of—even because of—our inadequacies, so that God can bring about through us what he is asking of us at this moment in our lives. That's the point.

Jack Mahoney SJ,
Glimpses of the Gospels

'He Fell on His Neck and Kissed Him'

Few things in life are certain, but one of the certainties of life is this: we will make mistakes. We will make a lot of mistakes. Early in life we often feel guilty and ashamed of our mistakes, perhaps thinking that we are the only ones who make them. As we grow older, however, we see that making mistakes—messing things up and failure—is part of life for everyone. While mistakes are not to be sought out, they are not the end of the story.

Mistakes are to be learned from and grown out of. They are opportunities for us to sheepishly, maybe, and humbly, definitively, turn back to God in search of the forgiveness or strength that will inevitably await us and help us to move on along a better path. One of the best lines in the New Testament dealing with failure comes in the story of the Prodigal Son, or the Forgiving Father, as it is increasingly known. When the wayward son, who has really messed up, comes back to his father seeking forgiveness for his mistakes, we read the following about the father's reaction to the son: 'He fell on his neck and kissed him.'

How wonderful to have a God who falls on our neck and kisses us when we mess up and ask for his forgiveness! And what better way to be his presence in the world than to do the same for others in our lives?

Brendan McManus SJ and Jim Deeds,
Deeper in the Mess: Conversations with God

LENT

Lent

Introduction to Lent

It seems that we are somehow programmed to begin again and again. This is true at the level of nature: springtime is precisely the time of new life, sprung from the dark earth of winter. It is also true at the spiritual level for us as believers: we are reborn, a new creation in Christ. 'He is the head of the body, the church; he is the beginning, the firstborn from the dead, so that he might come to have first place in everything' (Colossians 1:18). The springtime of faith—Lent means springtime—calls us to a new and deeper engagement with our God, whose mercies are new every morning, as we read in the Book of Lamentations: 'The steadfast love of the LORD never ceases, his mercies never come to an end; they are new every morning; great is your faithfulness' (Lamentations 3:22–23). The Lent lectionary is perhaps the most considered and the richest. This is right, surely, because the season guides us as pilgrims to the great festival of Easter.

As in farming and gardening, there is work to be done if this new growth is to flourish or even to happen at all. We have to look back and see what has done well and what has, in effect, died off. We need to make space by clearing the ground and looking at ourselves honestly. It would be good to identify what will feed and sustain us during this journey from the ashes of Ash Wednesday to the new birth of Easter.

The insistent demand to begin again in our time is felt most urgently as we face global warming, the loss of species, the exploitation of earth's resources and an existential crisis for every human being and for humanity as a whole. We—all of us—simply cannot carry on as before, as if resources were somehow endless. As we learned through the difficult experience of the pandemic, the well-being of each is to be found in the well-being of all. Here is real and needed conversion—*metanoia*—for our time, a conversion that is at once moral, existential, social and spiritual.

Kieran O'Mahony,
Hearers of the Word:
Praying & Exploring the Readings
for Lent & Holy Week, Year C

Lenten Reflections

Living with Reality

A friend of mine from the Lutheran tradition has a very interesting question about Catholic Lent. 'Why do you need to do these things once a year—why don't you do all these good things all year?' I must say I had no answer.

When you cut to the quick, there is no doubt that for a Christian the entire year should be Lenten in spirit, but we are frail people and we need a good kick in the backside every so often, and an opportunity to benefit from that self-same kick. In fact, many of the great spiritual writers would hold the view that we should have a Lenten mindset all year round.

Some of these same writers would point out that Lent falls at a time of year when the pantry is running low. When the pantry was all you had, there was a sense of 'making do' until spring produced fresh produce. Lent helped this process. Rather than Lent being an occasion to make a personal decision to give something up it was a chance to live with the reality that the resources of the earth are scarce, and that we live in a fragile world.

Alan Hilliard,
Dipping into Lent

St Patrick

I often wonder how St Patrick would describe himself. Did he see himself as a constant migrant? Did he come back to Ireland because he felt an affinity with the people? Was he aware of the fluidity of the world of his time, prompted by trade and transport not unlike globalisation today? Did he feel constrained in his own place among his family and community? Was he just plain restless? Did his early experience of slavery discommode him? Was he someone who rose above tribal identity and found his identity in his work and his belief?

All these questions lead us to both wonder and understand how St Patrick is relevant to us today. For many years, religious faith in Ireland gave us a sense of belonging. Many identified themselves with the school they went to, the parish they attended or their college. Today, identity is changing because our world is changing. St Patrick is a good model for us in this age of globalisation and seemingly endless emphasis on nationalism and sovereignty. As someone who, we believe, lived in a number of places often against his will, his identity lay beyond what geographical borders dictate. It was from his struggling heart that prayers like this took shape:

May the Strength of God guide us.
May the Power of God preserve us.
May the Wisdom of God instruct us.
May the Hand of God protect us.
May the Way of God direct us.
May the Shield of God defend us.
May the Angels of God guard us
against the snares of the evil one.

May Christ be with us!
May Christ be before us!
May Christ be in us,
Christ be over all!

May Thy Grace, Lord,
always be ours,
this day, O Lord, and for evermore.
Amen.

Alan Hilliard,
Dipping into Lent

People of the Transfiguration

The big truth of Jesus is that he is intimately united to God the Father. So following him is not just action, but prayer that leads to action. We say someone is a great Christian—he or she helps the poor. Christianity is more—it is also prayer and the Eucharist. While we are thankful for the good lives of many people, we also can say that the full Christian life includes prayer and Mass.

It also involves community—the three were called to witness and help each other remember the Lord Jesus. Community brings the word of God alive in a real way. The community of the Church brings us to fuller faith.

Prayer leads to action for others, and action leads back to prayer. We can be so close to heavenly things that we are no earthly good! Lent brings us into this mystery of the death and resurrection of the Lord—we are part of this, and we try to make life a grace for others. We can transfigure or disfigure the lives of others. Let's be people of the transfiguration.

Donal Neary SJ,
Gospel Reflections for Sundays of Year C

This Is Good News!

My father, God rest him, had an accident many years ago and, as a result, lost the sight in one eye. In his later years, the sight in the other eye began to deteriorate. It was decided that he needed to have a cataract removed and the appointment was given for 7:45 am on Good Friday. My niece and I took him to Sligo General for the procedure. It was a lovely morning, clear skies and all was well, but he told me he didn't know how I was able to drive in such an awful fog. This made me aware of what he was looking through. Though the day was perfectly clear, his view of it was through a heavy fog. There was no doubt he needed the surgery!

The procedure was relatively fast and simple and shortly after 9:00 am he was ready to go home, but his eye was bandaged, and he was now completely blind and dependent on us. We guided him as best we could to the car, got him in and headed for home. I told him where we were along the way—Ballymote, Gurteen, Mullaghroe and home. We helped him from the car and took him to the sitting-room. The fog of morning was now total darkness for him. He spent the rest of Good Friday like that.

On Holy Saturday I went home. He was unbandaged but felt there was grit in his eye, and he was in some discomfort. He was okay but a bit down. He knew, as we all did, that there was always a slight possibility that things might not work out. It is possible that he was thinking of this on Saturday. We reassured him that he would improve and, though he agreed, he looked very vulnerable and was, I'm certain, more than a little worried.

On Easter Sunday morning, I got a text message sent shortly after 7:00 am from my brother. He had gone home and found my father at the kitchen table, sitting there and reading an old parish bulletin. Yes, reading, and doing so without glasses. He told my brother he had weighed himself and was three pounds lighter than my niece had told him. He could see the scales. My brother's text concluded, 'I hope I did not wake you, but this is good news!' So it was, and so it remains!

There seems to me to be a link in the move from Good Friday to Easter Sunday. My father's Good Friday began in a cloud, moved into darkness that lasted through Friday and Saturday. Easter Sunday morning brought new sight and light and, as my brother so rightly said, 'Good News'.

Vincent Sherlock,
Celebrating Holy Week

Palm Sunday

There are two parades of Holy Week. First, into Jerusalem from Bethany on the Sunday and Jesus being acclaimed as a political saviour. People hoped he would triumph, that his followers would put him into power, and he would get rid of the Romans.

The second, from Jerusalem, outside the walls of the city on the following Friday, to Calvary; a man in disgrace. A man carrying his cross, crowned with thorns, mocked, bullied and tortured. About to be killed. Like the parade to a dishonoured graveside.

He had all sorts of followers—some like camp followers, some terrorists, some people on the make for themselves. There were also the ones who stayed until the end, like his mother, an aunt and a few loyal friends. Others stayed at a distance, but they would come back, and, later, would follow to the end.

We hope to be in that second parade.

Palms are for waving in triumph; then they wither. The cross is forever, for all time.

The cross is his love, and as we follow in this parade we show our willingness to console him in love to the end.

This is a holy week because a man like us, and one of the Trinity, gave his life.

Donal Neary SJ,
Gospel Reflections for Sundays of Year B

The Last Supper

Did you ever think about the man carrying the pitcher of water in Mark 14:12–16? It would be a pity to overlook him on a day like today. We are not told much, indeed anything, about him as a person, but he is a key figure. Jesus had told his disciples, 'You will see a man carrying a pitcher of water', and that they should follow him to the house where he was going. You would wonder about him. How many times he must have filled that pitcher, countless times in truth, and walked the street back to the house. That day was different though. His everyday task became a sign, a sacrament perhaps, and his role in this ever-unfolding drama took centre stage. He was noticed! There is something about noticing people, not least when they do not expect it, and it is linked with noticing the difference they make.

Holy Thursday calls us to a place of awareness around Eucharist and service. These two are centre stage in all that is happening today. We are asked to be aware of people around us, to notice people, not just for the sake of noticing but because otherwise they might all too easily go unnoticed.

In this evening's Liturgy, there will be witness given to the Lord's call to be servants of one another. This, we are told, he did in the washing of his disciples' feet. They were reluctant to have this done, especially so Peter, who said, 'You will never wash my feet' (John 13:8). When Jesus pointed out that if he did not allow this to happen then Peter could have nothing to do with his ministry, he changed his mind saying, 'Lord, not my feet only but also my hands and head!' (John 13:9)—that response, that change of attitude, is perhaps central to our approach to a moment like this. The willingness to be open to a new message and take on a role not imagined is at once challenging and exciting.

Where did Jesus get the water to wash the disciples' feet? Certainly, it is possible that it is some of that same water carried by the man with the pitcher. That water too, finished up beside the wine on the table and may well have been mixed with it, as we see time and time again when the bread and wine are offered at the altar. Noticing! That's the best gift you can bring to this day. Noticing! Noticing people, noticing signs, noticing what is done around the altar and noticing the people involved and those, like the man who carried the water, who may well be behind the scenes. Noticing!

Notice the ending of Mass tonight. There will be no final blessing; the priest will leave the altar in silence with no closing hymn. He may well carry the Eucharist to an 'Altar of Repose' where adoration might continue for a number of hours but there is no formal ending or dismissal. This is because the prayer is truly only begun and will continue through Good Friday, Holy Saturday and all the way to the discovery of the empty tomb on Easter Sunday morning. It is great that you are here. It is where you need to be and where you are needed.

Vincent Sherlock,
Celebrating Holy Week

An Example to Follow

[Jesus] has been betrayed, cast aside and rejected by most of humanity. He has suffered the most awful physical and emotional torture. He can see no way forward and cries out to his Father to rescue him from the ignominy of the cross. This must be one of the most heartfelt cries of anguish or loneliness that must ever have been heard on the face of the earth; it will have gone right to the heart of God. However, Jesus acknowledges his son-ship and wishes to uphold the mission of the Father for the salvation of the world. He surrenders his own will to the will of the Father and in this he finds the courage to go on, to complete the salvation story and to win true peace for himself and all humankind.

In this he has left us an example to follow—when our wills are in union with the will of the Father, we too receive the grace to live through any loneliness and to come to a new and deeper peace at the core of our souls.

Siobhán O'Keeffe SHJM,
I Am with You Always

Lenten Retreat

Introduction

The season of Lent gives us a heaven-sent opportunity to reflect prayerfully on our recent experience and the difficulties and the possibilities it has set before us.

Each of us has our own personal role to play in the great story of transformation. 'Transformation', we might well think, is not for us little people. Saints and heroes do transformation, not humble pilgrims on a rocky road. Actually, the very opposite is the truth. Transformation happens one pilgrim at a time, step by painful step, precisely on the rocky roads of life. The Gospel gives us both a vision and a map for this journey.

We are making this journey personally, but we are also making it together as the human family. However I would like to introduce you to a particular fellow pilgrim who will be accompanying us on our Lenten journey. You may already be very familiar with him, or perhaps you may never have heard of him. It doesn't matter—he won't hold that against you. His name is Ignatius of Loyola, but during this retreat we will refer to him simply as Iñigo. Iñigo fought his own battles with the challenge of transformation, half a millennium ago, and he was inspired to make notes about his inner journey with its many gifts and graces, but also its times of temptation and despair. These notes formed the basis of his *Spiritual Exercises*. What is not always realised is that Iñigo was a lay person when he was making this momentous, and ultimately world-changing, journey and formulating his Exercises. They have guided many millions of spiritual searchers through the intervening ages, and they resonate deeply and remarkably with twenty-first-century psychology and spirituality.

The first thing Iñigo would want to tell us is this: 'Don't follow me. Follow the One I follow.' Ignatian spirituality is completely Christ-centred and Gospel-guided. It gives us a kind of spiritual toolkit to help us make the gospel journey in very practical, accessible ways. We will be using this toolkit extensively during our retreat. It opens up ways of reflecting on where we find ourselves in our relationship with God, and how we might begin to walk more closely in the footsteps of Jesus, learning from him, like apprentices, seeking to internalise his values and wisdom into our own lives. The journey will take us, as it did him, into the darkest places of Holy Week and then beyond them to the joy of a new dawn at Easter. Above all it will ask us the searching question, 'What is Love asking of you now, in the place, time and circumstances in which you find yourself?'

As you take these issues into prayer Iñigo would urge you to shape a daily prayer routine that works for you, and includes:

- Reflecting on what you are asking of God today— what gift or grace do you especially seek? Jesus once asked a blind man, 'What do you want me to do for you?' (Luke 18:41). The blind man asked that he might see again. Think about how you would respond to this question yourself. Perhaps you too are seeking clearer vision in some aspect of your life?

- Taking some time each day (perhaps 10–15 minutes) to look back over how the day has been. This form of prayer is often called the Examen or, simply, Review of the Day, and Iñigo urged his companions never to neglect it even if they had no time for any other form of prayer. This isn't a blow-by-blow re-run of the day, but simply a matter of relaxing into God's presence and recalling what has most moved you, challenged you, disturbed or consoled you. Where has God been in the day's events? For what are you most grateful? Is there anything that, on reflection, you wish you had done differently, or not done at all?

Simply bring it all into prayer, without judging yourself, or anyone else, and ask for the light of the Holy Spirit to show you whatever God wants you to see.

As you spend time with the Scripture text suggested for each session, use any form of prayer that helps you—perhaps the prayer of the listening heart (*lectio divina*), or perhaps imagining yourself present at a particular scene (imaginative meditation) and opening your heart to whatever God wishes to reveal to you.

As you journey, you might also find it helpful to keep your own notes, in the form of a journal or diary, noting what is especially firing your heart and capturing your attention, what grace the week has brought you and how you have been challenged or encouraged. This doesn't have to be a work of literature—in fact it shouldn't be—but just your own honest feelings about where your prayer is leading you. Some people may prefer to do this using a sketchpad and images instead of words. It is a maxim of Ignatian spirituality to use whatever helps you to come closer to God, and leave aside anything that is not helpful.

May these weeks of Lent lead us all ever closer to God, to each other and to all God's creatures, and to the deep and sacred source of our own being.

LENTEN RETREAT: SESSION 1
Where is My Life Centred?

Invitation to Stillness

Take a moment to become still as you begin this session:

Wherever you are, sitting, standing, inside, outside, take time to notice what is around you . . . what do you see? . . . what do you hear? . . . how is the air as you inhale through your nose? . . . how is your body in contact with your clothes, your chair or the ground? . . . how focused were you able to be as you were noticing? . . . notice that . . . let God look at you . . .

Reading

Job 38:1–11, 40:3–5

Then the Lord answered Job out of the
  whirlwind:
'Who is this that darkens counsel by words
  without knowledge?
Gird up your loins like a man,
I will question you, and you shall declare to me.

'Where were you when I laid the foundation of
  the earth?
Tell me, if you have understanding.
Who determined its measurements—surely you
  know!

Or who stretched the line upon it?
On what were its bases sunk,
or who laid its cornerstone
when morning stars sang together
and all the heavenly beings shouted for joy?

'Or who shut in the sea with doors
when it burst out from the womb? –
when I made the clouds its garment,
and thick darkness its swaddling band,
and prescribed bounds for it,
and set bars and doors,
and said, "Thus far shall you come, and no
    farther,
and here shall your proud waves be stopped"?'

Then Job answered the LORD:
'See, I am of small account; what shall I answer
    you?
I lay my hand on my mouth.
I have spoken once, and I will not answer;
twice, but will proceed no further.'

Reflect

- There is something about this encounter between God and Job that rings deeply true. It captures so much of human hubris, and our assumption that we can know and do and control everything.

God speaks to Job 'out of the whirlwind'. Is God speaking today out of *our* whirlwind?

- God, it seems, has had enough of 'know-alls' and confronts Job with two chapters' worth of challenging questions that could possibly be summed up in the words 'Who do you actually think you are?'

- Indeed, God's description of divine control over the limits of the ocean could well be applied to ourselves and our recent experience of being globally stopped in our tracks: 'Thus far you shall come, and no farther. Here shall your proud waves be stopped.'

- Job's response is actually very touching. Utterly humbled, he realises just how small he really is and agrees to be less vocal and more ready to listen in the future.

- During this retreat we are on a journey towards transformation, but it begins at the bottom, not the top of the mountain. At the beginning of his *Spiritual Exercises*, Iñigo urges us to spend time reflecting on where we truly find ourselves, and to take on board the revolutionary truth that creation does not exist to serve us and our egos, and is not under our control, but that all creation, including our own hearts and minds, can only find purpose and fulfilment when in right relationship with the deeper centre. We will 'grow back better' only if our lives are rooted in this deeper centre.

- Take some time this week to reflect on what this means for you personally. A good question to keep returning to might be: 'In this situation, am I really trying to make events revolve around my own ego or am I focused on a deeper centre?'

- Don't be disheartened. We are all ego-centred much of the time, but to recognise this pattern of thinking and behaving is a sign that, deep down, we desire for it to be otherwise. Once recognised, we can ask for the grace to be more aware of our spiritual orientation (God-directed or ego-directed) in any given circumstances, and for the courage and humility to begin the process of change.

Talk to God

As you look back over the week, do you recognise any incidents or conversations in which you can now see that you were trying, perhaps unconsciously, to make things 'go your way'? How do you feel about them now? Such moments often leave us with a sense of unease. If this is your experience, can you express your feelings in prayer?

On the other hand there will have been incidents or conversations which, on reflection, seem to you to have been grounded in a deeper centre, a God-centre. How do you feel about these incidents in hindsight? Such moments usually leave us with a sense of inner peace, even though the circumstances may have been challenging.

Make a note in your journal of anything that has felt especially important to you this week. Notice those moments when you felt 'God-centred' and how you responded to this grace.

As we begin to recognise, like Job, that we really know very little and understand less, can we come to God in this genuine humility, and ask for the grace to begin this journey, trusting less in our own powers while remaining more open to the guidance of the Holy Spirit?

LENTEN RETREAT: SESSION 2
Living in Balance

Invitation to Stillness

Take a moment to become still as you begin this session:

Pay attention to your breathing, without changing the rhythm. Notice your breathing in . . . and your breathing out . . . notice the rhythm . . . the depth . . . the feel of the air entering and leaving your mouth or nose . . . take three deeper breaths . . .

Reading

John 12:23–26

Jesus answered them, 'The hour has come for the Son of Man to be glorified. Very truly, I tell you, unless a grain of wheat falls into the earth and dies, it remains just a single grain; but if it dies, it bears much fruit. Those who love their life lose it, and those who hate their life in this world will keep it for eternal life. Whoever serves me must follow me, and where I am, there will my servant be also. Whoever serves me, the Father will honour.'

Reflect

- This is one of the sayings attributed to Jesus that sounds preposterous. It runs counter to all our instincts, as well as to contemporary psychological insights, to 'hate our life in this world' not to mention the apparent promise that if we hate our life enough, we will get to keep it for ever.

- Yet this strange warning in today's reading is actually a powerful key to the mystery of what Ignatian spirituality calls *detachment*. The word detachment can appear to imply a kind of separatist indifference towards the rest of the world and the needs of others. Actually, in terms of spirituality, it means pretty much the opposite of this. It might be better expressed as the art of being at balance with all that happens, so that we are not pulled off track either by triumph or disaster, but able, in the words of Rudyard Kipling, 'to treat those two imposters just the same', by refusing to let them take over our consciousness.

- If there is something (or someone) we either inordinately desire to possess or inordinately desire to avoid, such an attachment robs us of our inner freedom, and we can become enslaved by it. God invites us to make choices that are not shaped either by the hope of gain or the fear of loss, but spring from the deepest part of our heart, where God is indwelling.

- The secret really is about sitting lightly enough in relation to all created things and circumstances so that we are not seduced by them into making choices contrary to our deepest values. It's about gratefully enjoying these gifts while we have them, but not falling apart if we lose them, so that nothing on earth has the power to undermine our spiritual equilibrium.

- Iñigo learned this lesson the hard way, through the bitter experience of his own vulnerability and compulsions and even, on occasion, his despair. We are not alone as we walk this rocky road.

- This reading is also crucial to our journey to transformation because of its striking image of the seed falling into the ground and dying before the new life it contains can emerge. We all know from the natural world that this is the way life renews itself, but it is harder to take on board that something in ourselves or in our society or world order also has to die if we are to be free to move on to the next stage of our journey. To allow this process to happen requires of us that we release our possessive grip on these things sufficiently to allow them to die when the time is right.

- In the course of our lives we will have to let a great deal go, including quite possibly our livelihoods, our health, our mobility, our faculties, our financial security, our independence and, finally, physical life itself. The process of detachment is an ongoing challenge. Jesus warns us about it, but also teaches us how to embrace it and accompanies us through it by experiencing so many human losses in his own earthly life.

Talk to God

Take a long hard look this week at your own life. Is there anything you are clinging to excessively or feel you couldn't live without? Anything you are determined to gain or achieve at all costs? Anything you are afraid of facing to the extent that you make every effort to avoid it? The call to detachment invites you to relax your grip on any earthly goal that is tending to take over your consciousness, and then enjoy the freedom to make your life choices from a point of inner balance.

Sometimes the good can be the enemy of the better. Is there any aspect of your own life that, though it may feel good, needs to be let go, to allow something better to emerge? The experience of global crisis is stripping all of us of many of our previous securities. Is this a time during which our human 'grain of wheat' is falling into the ground and dying? Can you trust that this 'dying' is the necessary pre-condition for the emergence of new life? Could what we see as a threat to our well-being become a way through to our *better*-being? What are your own hopes for how that human better-being might look?

The last part of today's reading is a very clear instruction: to serve, and to follow. As we move on in our Lenten journey, we will discover more of what it means to serve God and each other, and to follow Jesus in order to walk the path of love. Note that Jesus repeatedly asks us to follow him, not to worship, but to follow, not just to talk, but to walk the talk. What does this call mean to you personally?

Make a note in your journal of anything you have learned from your prayer this week, anything you may be clinging to, or are afraid of, or anything that you feel has, like the seed, died and fallen into the ground. We might, this week, pray for the grace to recognise and embrace our own vulnerability, trusting that the dying of the seed of all we think we are can release the new growth of all we can become.

LENTEN RETREAT: SESSION 3
Sailing into Deeper Water

Invitation to Stillness

Take a moment to become still as you begin this session:

Call to mind any concerns you have been carrying recently . . . as you breathe out, share them with God . . . you might even be able to hand some of these over, at least for now . . . as you breathe out, hand them over to God . . . each time you breathe in, breathe in God's love for you . . . let it fill your body . . . take three deeper breaths . . .

Reading

Luke 5:1–6, 10–11

Once while Jesus was standing beside the Lake of Gennesaret, and the crowd was pressing in on him to hear the word of God, he saw two boats there at the shore of the lake; the fishermen had gone out of them and were washing their nets. He got into one of the boats, the one belonging to Simon, and asked him to put out a little way from the shore. Then he sat down and taught the crowds from the boat. When he had finished speaking, he said to Simon, 'Put out into the deep water and let down your nets for a catch.' Simon answered, 'Master, we have worked all night long but have caught nothing. Yet if you say so, I will let down the nets.' When they had done this, they caught so many fish that their nets were beginning to break. . . . Then Jesus said to Simon, 'Do not be afraid; from now on you will be catching people.' When they had brought their boats to shore, they left everything and followed him.

Reflect

- The next stage of our Lenten journey, and our life journey towards the best we can be, can be expressed in just two words: 'Follow me.' Our response to this call will take a lifetime and is subject to daily renewal. Iñigo accompanies us along the way in what he calls the Second Week of his Exercises, during which he invites us to follow Jesus more and more closely by entering ever more deeply and personally into the Gospel. Today's reading offers us a powerful and compelling 'launch' into this stage of our journey.

- In fact 'launch' is exactly what happens when Jesus encounters the fishermen on the lakeside. He first finds the empty boats, and then discovers the fishermen taking a bit of a break to wash their nets. Have you ever wondered how and where he might find *you*? Perhaps your spiritual boat is also moored at the lakeside while you, quite legitimately, get on with the chores of daily life. This interlude is about to be dramatically changed, however. Jesus steps right into Simon's empty boat. Just take a moment to reflect on how that might feel—if Jesus were to step right into *your* life's boat. Just when you think you have everything under control, along comes this captivating, enigmatic stranger who steps right in.

- He then proceeds to tell you where to sail—first a little distance from the shore, so that he can better address the crowds that are gathering, and then the very challenging request to put out their nets into deeper water. What he appears not to know is that you have been trying, and failing, to catch fish all night. How do you think you would have reacted to Jesus' words? Simon protests, but nevertheless does as Jesus asks.

- We are being invited to put out into deeper water too. Each of us will find ourselves called to take our inner journey further, to go beyond the boundaries we may have set for ourselves. Following Jesus will never allow us to stay safely in our comfort zone. Following is always an active verb. It's about learning, moving and growing. For the human family as a whole the invitation is to grow beyond our present limitations and risk both the pain and the promise of growth and transformation. It is wisely said that you will never discover new lands if you don't leave the harbour. We will not discover the 'better' we long for unless we risk sailing into deeper water.

• The reading ends with Jesus' promise that from now on they will become fishers of people. In a memorable sermon I once heard, the minister said this: 'Jesus invited them to become fishers of people because they were already fishers of fish.' In other words, God's call to us invites us to use the skills, talents and experience we already have. The minister went on to ask: 'What would Jesus have said to *you*?' What personal gifts and abilities are you being asked to bring to this great adventure of transformation?

Talk to God

Perhaps the story of the call of the fishermen fails to capture your imagination because you have no interest in angling. If so, how would you respond to the question: 'How is Jesus inviting *you* to follow him?' What talents, interests and experience do you have that he needs for his mission?

Do you perhaps feel that your spiritual journey is stuck on the shoreline or in the shallow waters?

Perhaps there are just too many nets to wash and not enough time to sail? Can you imagine Jesus stepping into your 'boat' and asking you to set sail again? How would you respond?

You might, this week, bring to prayer the invitation to 'put out into deeper water.' How does this call feel to you? What, specifically, does 'deeper water' mean to you in the context of your inner journey?

Could it be that the entire human family is being called to sail into deeper water as we strive to become more fully and truly human? What might this mean? What 'fish' might we discover in the deeper waters?

Make a note in your journal of anything that has struck you particularly this week, and how you feel God may be calling you to sail into deeper water. Try to express your response in either words or pictures.

As we reflect on the many layers of Jesus' call, we might pray this week for the grace to understand what his call means to each of us, and for all of us, and for the courage to follow him, wherever he leads.

LENTEN RETREAT: SESSION 4
Eyes to See, Ears to Hear

Invitation to Stillness

Take a moment to become still as you begin this session:

Assuming you are sitting, do a body scan . . . be aware of your feet on the floor and how they feel . . . of your legs touched by your clothes . . . by the chair supporting you . . . your lower back . . . upper back . . . shoulders . . . as you go through, notice if you're carrying any tension and let some of it go . . . your neck . . . head . . . face . . . we often carry tension in our face, so notice if you are and allow more relaxation to come . . . in your forehead . . . around the eyes . . . the jaw . . . the mouth . . . don't try too hard to relax or you won't be relaxed! . . . but come as you are. . . .

Reading

Matthew 13:10–15

Then the disciples came and asked him, 'Why do you speak to them in parables?' He answered, 'To you it has been given to know the secrets of the kingdom of heaven, but to them it has not been given. For to those who have, will more be given, and they will have an abundance but from those who have nothing, even what they have will be taken away.

The reason I speak to them in parables is that 'seeing they do not perceive, and hearing they do not listen, nor do they understand.' With them indeed is fulfilled the prophecy of Isaiah that says:

"You will indeed listen, but never understand, and you will indeed look, but never perceive.

For this people's heart has grown dull, and their ears are hard of hearing, and they have shut their eyes; so that they might not look with their eyes, and listen with their ears, and understand with their heart and turn—and I would heal them."

Reflect

- We live in an age of information overload. One unfortunate side-effect of this is that, out of the bombardment of messaging that constantly demands our attention, we need to be very selective in what we notice. Jesus' reproach could certainly apply to us in our times. Yet today's reading also promises that 'I would heal them.'

- In today's world it is genuinely necessary to 'switch off' to a great deal that presents itself, in the media, on social media and even in some personal interactions. Much that swirls around the channels of communication is at best irrelevant or negative, and at worst downright untrue or hate-filled. We need to filter it out, otherwise it can flood our consciousness and influence our choices and actions. As a result, it may well be that our hearts have grown dull, our eyes unseeing and our ears deaf.

- However, our companion Iñigo is a very practical pilgrim, always able to connect our spiritual vision to our everyday problems. He has a spiritual tool-kit which contains an invaluable aid to help us sharpen our perception, focus our inner vision, unblock our inner ears, and open up our hearts to what really matters. This is the tool of spiritual discernment and it is a key element of Ignatian spirituality. Using this tool takes practice—ideally it takes daily practice, using the prayer of the review of the day to notice what we are really seeing, hearing and experiencing in our daily lives, and how we are responding.

- The practice of discernment challenges us to see what is often concealed, and hear what is often unspoken, submerged in the tide of information that threatens to overwhelm us. The secret of tuning into this deeper listening and clearer sight is to make a habit of coming to stillness for a while each day, asking for the grace of ears that truly listen, and eyes that see the world through the lens of the heart. How might you nourish the habit of stillness and reflective awareness this week?

- The art of discernment is also very much about focus. What we focus on, feeding it by giving it our energy and attention, will grow. What we refuse to feed, by withdrawing our energy and attention from it, will shrink. A simple question therefore is: What aspects of our lives and our world do we want to grow and strengthen? We can help this to happen by feeding them with our focused attention. What aspects of ourselves and our world would we want to shrink? We help this to happen by starving them of our energy and attention. Today this is often expressed as 'giving oxygen' to certain issues or people. When we give oxygen to what is life-giving, it grows and thrives. When we give oxygen to what is negative and destructive, it feeds the flames of division and hatred like a forest fire.

Talk to God

The kingdom of heaven in our human lives is a bit like a plant: if it is to grow into the 'better' we long for, we need to feed it and be lovingly aware of what it needs. Or it is like a child. If she is to develop into her full potential, she needs us to feed her inner self by listening to what matters to her and nourishing her with loving attention. We don't feed our houseplants with toxic waste, or our children with hateful gossip. We help them to grow by caring for them and becoming daily more tuned in to what they really need.

How will you feed the kingdom of heaven this week? How will you help it to grow? How will you avoid doing or saying anything that might harm or diminish it?

What in particular has attracted your attention and energy this week? Has it opened your eyes to see something important? Perhaps the loneliness or heartache of a neighbour, or the practical needs of a friend who has lost her job, or the quiet wisdom of an elder you haven't taken time to listen to?

What have you been hearing this week amid the bustle of busyness and the clamour of conflicting news reports? Have you heard the quiet cry of the homeless living on our streets, or the exhausted sighs of over-worked healthcare workers, or the mute desperation of those who are living in deprivation or fear—desperation that is often expressed in the language of rage and fury?

Make a note in your journal of anything you have learned this week to help you make wiser choices and grow your part of God's dream for humanity.

God is longing to heal us of our inner blindness and deafness. Dare we ask this week for the grace to let God open our eyes, our ears and our hearts to see and hear and understand how we can make personal choices that help the kingdom grow and humanity become the best we can be?

LENTEN RETREAT: SESSION 5
New Life Merging out of Death

Invitation to Stillness

Take a moment to become still as you begin this session:

Assuming you're alone and sitting and able to stand up, do something with your body . . . if you're in a public space or outside, micromovements, or even imagining this happening instead will be fine . . . begin by standing up . . . let your back straighten and breathe in . . . keep breathing normally . . . what posture expresses how you are feeling today? . . . adopt that posture . . . let God look at you or be with you in any way that God wants . . . stay with that focus . . . how is God wanting you to move your body? . . . allow that to happen . . . let God look at you a bit longer . . . and return to your chair. . . .

Reading

John 11:17–19, 38–44

When Jesus arrived, he found that Lazarus had already been in the tomb for four days. Now Bethany was near Jerusalem, some two miles away, and many of the Jews had come to Martha and Mary to console them about their brother. . . . Then Jesus, again greatly disturbed, came to the tomb. It was a cave, and a stone was lying against it. Jesus said, 'Take away the stone.' Martha, the sister of the dead man, said to him, 'Lord, already there is a stench because he has been dead for four days.' Jesus said to her, 'Did I not tell you that if you believed, you would see the glory of God?' So they took away the stone. And Jesus looked upward and said, 'Father, I thank you for having heard me. I knew that you always hear me, but I have said this for the sake of the crowd standing here, so that they may believe that you sent me.' When he had said this, he cried with a loud voice, 'Lazarus, come out!' The dead man came out, his hands and feet bound with strips of cloth, and his face wrapped in a cloth. Jesus said to them, 'Unbind him, and let him go.'

Reflect

- As we journey through Lent we come closer to the time of Jesus' suffering and death, a time that is foreshadowed by the events in Bethany recorded in today's reading. Jesus and his friends had been travelling towards Jerusalem for the Passover festival when their journey was interrupted by a messenger bringing the news that Jesus' dear friend Lazarus was critically ill. There is a curious delay between Jesus receiving this news and actually arriving in Bethany—a delay during which he promises, enigmatically, that this sickness will not end in death but will reveal the greater glory of God. Yet, when he arrives in Bethany, Lazarus has already been dead and buried for four days.

- When you make the Spiritual Exercises you will be invited by Iñigo, and your guide, to spend some time 'in the tomb'. This will be a day or a few days spent being utterly empty before God and willing to wait in the darkness. Iñigo knew this experience of emptiness in his own life, and also discovered for himself that new things grow in the darkness and that the tomb is like a chrysalis, holding at its heart the potential for transformation.

- The events that follow are punctuated by three powerful commands issued by Jesus, the first to Lazarus's sister Martha, the second to Lazarus himself and the third to all those in the crowd that had gathered. Are they also commands to us in our own lives?

- Jesus first tells the distraught Martha to 'take away the stone', prefiguring the miraculous rolling away of the stone that would cover his own tomb a few days later. She protests. It seems like an impossible thing to do, but Jesus insists. What immovable stones seem to be blocking our own path into the future we long to build for ourselves and for our Earth and all her creatures?

- Once the stone has been removed Jesus calls out to Lazarus with the command to 'Come out.' Is Jesus calling us out of some tomb or captivity of our own? What is keeping us inwardly paralysed and preventing us from embracing the fullness of life that God is offering?

- And finally, Jesus tells the bystanders to 'unbind him'. Lazarus is tightly wrapped up in a shroud. Unless he is liberated from this binding, he isn't going anywhere. Is God asking us to help 'unbind' each other, to help each other towards the liberation we all long for? None of us can be freed through our own efforts. We need God and we need each other.

- In German the word for 'unbind' is '*entbinden*', which gives a whole extra layer of meaning to this command. *Entbinden*, in German, mainly means to give birth. Birthing requires midwives. The shroud of death will become the swaddling clothes of new life. Are we being asked to be midwives to each other as, slowly and painfully, the fullness of the people we are created to be is coming to birth? Are we being asked to give birth to the 'better' on planet Earth?

Talk to God

For many people the future is blocked by what seem to be immovable stones—stones such as poverty, exploitation, modern slavery, prejudice, armed conflict and every kind of injustice that causes those who are powerless and voiceless to be marginalised. These are very big boulders. None of us can move them using our own strength alone, yet each of us can add our own strength to the effort. Maybe this week reflect on the stones you see in the world around you, and ask yourself whether there is anything you can do, along with others, to begin to move them.

Reflect on any kind of entombment or confinement you may be living in yourself. What is preventing you from leaving the apparent safety of your 'tomb' and risking the bright dawn of a new beginning? What might Jesus' command to 'come out' mean for you personally?

All around you, new life is striving to come to birth, but it needs a midwife to unbind the shroud that confines it. Is there someone who needs your help to be unbound? Perhaps a listening ear to help free someone from crippling fears, or to really hear their voice that has been silenced for too long and no longer trusts itself to speak? What does Jesus' command to 'unbind' mean to you?

Make a note in your journal of your own experience of being 'entombed', perhaps of the stones that keep you in your tomb or your response to the call to 'come out'. Try expressing, in words or pictures, anything that is 'binding' you.

In the Third Week of his Exercises, Iñigo invites us to journey with Jesus through his suffering and death. The story of Lazarus challenges us to recognise what love is asking of us as we journey together through the darkness. Lazarus's sickness does not end in death. It is the precursor of new life. May we have the grace this week to trust that promise and be given the courage to make this journey alongside Jesus and alongside each other.

LENTEN RETREAT: SESSION 6
Journeying through the Darkness

Invitation to Stillness

Take a moment to become still as you begin this session:

As you come to the prayer today, notice what is on your mind . . . let each thought that comes drop away . . . notice how you are feeling at this moment . . . can you put names on your feelings? . . . can you locate where in your body they are? . . . notice how you are in your body today . . . relaxed or tense . . . cold or warm . . . tired or wide awake . . . how is your body? . . . however you are, let God look at you with love and welcome you to this time together . . .

Reading

Matthew 27:15–25

Now at the festival the governor was accustomed to release a prisoner for the crowd, anyone whom they wanted. At that time they had a notorious prisoner, called Jesus Barabbas. So after they had gathered, Pilate said to them, 'Whom do you want me to release for you, Jesus Barabbas or Jesus who is called the Messiah? For he realised that it was out of jealousy that they had handed him over. While he was sitting on the judgement seat, his wife sent word to him, 'Have nothing to do with that innocent man, for today I have suffered a great deal because of a dream about him.' Now the chief priests and the elders persuaded the crowds to ask for Barabbas and to have Jesus killed. The governor again said to them, 'Which of the two do you want me to release for you?' And they said 'Barabbas.' Pilate said to them, 'Then what should I do with Jesus who is called the Messiah?' All of them said, 'Let him be crucified!' Then he asked, 'Why, what evil has he done?' But they shouted all the more, 'Let him be crucified!' So when Pilate saw that he could do nothing, but rather that a riot was beginning, he took some water and washed his hands before the crowd, saying, 'I am innocent of this man's blood; see to it yourselves.' Then the people as a whole answered, 'His blood be on us and on our children.'

Reflect

- As we walk alongside Jesus through the events of Holy Week we may find insights about ourselves as participants in this cosmic drama reflected back in many different ways. Iñigo invites us to enter into these events prayerfully throughout the Third Week of the Exercises, noticing which aspects touch something in our own lives and hearts, and to ask for the grace to listen to what God is saying to us personally.

- It is ironic that the outcome of this momentous week appears to lie in the hands of a fearful and indecisive human being, who nevertheless wields great secular power. When it comes to the fateful decision about what to do with Jesus, the buck stops with Pilate, as governor of the province. We find him here grappling with his conscience. He knows that Jesus is innocent. He knows that the demand to have Jesus killed is motivated by jealousy and the perceived threat he poses to official power. And, crucially, Pilate has been warned by his wife, who had been warned in a dream, not to have anything to do with this immoral act.

- We all face moral dilemmas in our lives. Sometimes the choices we make can derail another person's well-being or even their life, or affect the future of a whole community. We too may know, in our hearts, what is the right course to choose, but there are many things that can cause us to abdicate our moral responsibility. Pilate is afraid of triggering a riot and bringing the force of Rome down upon them all. You and I may not be in danger of causing a riot, but we may well shy away from upsetting our friends or family, neighbours or work colleagues. For many of us there may be a dread of confrontation, and a tendency to take the line of least resistance in any conflict situation.

- But Pilate has another source of guidance—his wife's dream. What might this dream be telling us today? You might want to take this into prayer and ask for the grace to recognise those deeper streams of guidance that are prompting your own heart to act justly. It isn't necessarily about dreams. It's about noticing those moments that we know are directing us to that source of truth in the core of our being, but these signposts are very easy to ignore when we are faced with the clamouring crowd of fears and insecurities triggered by the pressure of immediate circumstances.

- We recall how Pilate had famously asked Jesus, 'What is truth?' Now he has to decide whether the promptings of the dream or the demands of the crowd are the truth. He knows that Jesus is innocent. The crowd, however, whipped up into a frenzy, have convinced themselves that Jesus' guilt is the truth. 'Alternative facts', it appears, were as alive and active two thousand years ago as they are in our own times, fuelled by the same base motives of fear and jealousy and deliberately manipulated by the chief priests and elders. Who are 'the chief priests and elders' in our own times? Who are the opinion shapers and how are they manipulating *our* choices? Will we choose our future course, both personally and collectively, under the spell of covert propagandists and social media trolls, or under the guidance of the Holy Spirit?

• Finally, Pilate washes his hands of the matter. He abdicates his responsibility. He throws truth to the winds, and it is blown away, with tragic consequences. Are we also tempted to abdicate our personal responsibility for the direction the world will take? Do we think there's nothing we can do to change things? Jesus was never so apparently helpless as in the events of Holy Week, standing defenceless against the forces of evil—and yet never more powerful!

Talk to God

Bring to prayer any particular moral dilemmas you may be facing. Do you know deep down which course best reflects the truth that you know in your heart? Is anything working against that truth and tempting you to choose the line of least resistance?

Sometimes we find that the voice of the 'crowd'—the crowd of our fears and insecurities, or the crowd of peer pressure, for example—is very much louder and more forceful than the still small voice of truth in our hearts. Which voice do you truly desire to follow? Can you ask for the grace to have the courage of your deepest convictions in the choices that lie before you?

How aware are you of the insidious malicious persuaders in our times, people who are deliberately manipulating our choices as a human family for their own ends and to bolster their own power? These agents of persuasion are on a mission to undermine our quest, and our calling, to evolve into the best we can be, just as they attempted to subvert Jesus' mission of love and redemption. Can you ask for the grace to recognise them and act against them?

Make a note in your journal of any ways in which you recognise yourself in the reaction of Pilate or in any other part of the narrative of Holy Week. What do you feel this recognition is teaching you?

May we collectively ask for the grace to recognise the divine voice of authentic truth and resist all the malevolent fakes that surround us daily.

LENTEN RETREAT: SESSION 7
A New Day Dawns

Invitation to Stillness

Take a moment to become still as you begin this session:

Pay attention to your breathing, without changing the rhythm . . . notice your breathing in . . . and your breathing out . . . notice the rhythm . . . the depth . . . the feel of the air entering and leaving your mouth or nose . . . take three deeper breaths . . .

Reading

John 21:4–12

Just after daybreak, Jesus stood on the beach; but the disciples did not know that it was Jesus. Jesus said to them, 'Children, you have no fish, have you?' They answered him, 'No.' He said to them, 'Cast the net to the right side of the boat, and you will find some.' So they cast it, and now they were not able to haul it in because there were so many fish. That disciple whom Jesus loved said to Peter, 'It is the Lord!' When Simon Peter heard that it was the Lord, he put on some clothes, for he was naked, and jumped into the lake. But the other disciples came in the boat, dragging a net full of fish, for they were not far from the land, only about a hundred yards off.

When they came ashore, they saw a charcoal fire there, with fish on it, and bread. Jesus said to them, 'Bring some of the fish that you have just caught. So Simon Peter went aboard and hauled the net ashore, full of large fish, a hundred and fifty-three of them; and though there were so many, the net was not torn. Jesus said to them, 'Come and have breakfast.'

Reflect

- The disciples are traumatised. The friend they had believed would save the world has been brutally executed, and they themselves are known collaborators. In their desperation they have gone back to where it all began, back to fishing, but they have caught nothing. Even the lake reflects the sick emptiness in their hearts.

- However, the darkness of Good Friday and the emptiness of the tomb are about to give way to a new daybreak and an unexpected fullness. They notice a stranger on the shore.

- It's a feature of almost all the Resurrection appearances that, initially, the people to whom Jesus appears fail to recognise him. In this fishing boat on a sorrow-laden early morning, only one person recognises Jesus—the one 'whom Jesus loved'. This suggests that we will recognise the risen presence through the eyes of love, and when we open these inner eyes, we will find the signs of resurrection all around us.

- Iñigo leads us into the miracle of resurrection in the Fourth Week of his Exercises. He invites us to be present in prayer to the appearances of the risen Christ and to reflect on what resurrection means for us in our everyday lives. As always, our practical companion is eager for us to see resurrection not just as an historic event in which we believe, but as an ongoing dynamic reality calling and enabling us to live our lives to the fullest and truly grow back better from the trauma of the past.

- Earlier in our Lenten journey our life's 'boat' was launched when Jesus stepped into it and urged us to put out into deeper water. Now, as we draw close to the end of this journey together, he gives us another unexpected invitation—to put down our nets on the other side of the boat. This makes little sense by human logic. If there are no fish on one side of the boat why would there be fish—and in such overwhelming numbers—on the other side? But the disciples do as he suggests.

- Perhaps this instruction, as we reflect on it in our own prayer today, is actually inviting us to look at life from a radically different point of view.

Perhaps what we think is a stumbling block is really a stepping stone. Perhaps the person who gives us the most trouble is the piece of grit in our oyster that has the potential to become a pearl. Are we being asked to pray outside the box?

- But today's reading promises that the time of frustration and hopelessness is nearly over. Transformation has taken place in the tomb and has released a new energy, capable of transforming our world. This is also a promise that transformation can happen in our own experience of darkness, disappointment, and the death of our dreams, but it asks us to change our way of seeing things and cast our nets from the other side of the boat.

- But right now, a stranger we already know but don't easily recognise, is preparing a barbecue on the shore. Are we ready to join him for breakfast?

Talk to God

There are signs of resurrection all around us—in the kindness of strangers, in the faithfulness of those who care for the sick and the lonely, in the food banks and community volunteers, in the patience of teachers, in the simple exuberance of a child at play, in the quiet wisdom of an elderly friend, and in the new growth and changing seasons that our wounded earth continues to give us so unconditionally—in all of these and so many other ways, we meet the power of resurrection, and the spirit of the risen Christ. Where have you encountered the stranger on the shore this week?

What does it mean to you to 'cast your net from the other side of the boat'? Is there any issue or situation or relationship in your life that you feel God is asking you to see from a different perspective? Try holding up the mirror of prayer to this matter and see how it might look from the other side of your heart.

The time between Good Friday and Easter Sunday can feel like empty space, but it is precisely in this empty space that the miracle of transformation happens and new energy is released, like a butterfly from a chrysalis. Try bringing any places of emptiness in your own life consciously into the light of the Holy Spirit. These places are your own Holy Saturdays where transformation begins.

Make a note in your journal of any moments this week when you have glimpsed the power of resurrection. As you look into the mirror of prayer, try expressing what you see, either in words or pictures. Notice especially anything that takes you by surprise or overturns your expectations.

This week you might ask for the grace to see your circumstances through the eyes of love, recognise the light of resurrection already dawning in your life and in the world, have the courage to cross to the other side of the boat, and be open to God's surprises where you least expect to find them.

Conclusion

At the end of this Lenten journey, perhaps you have been challenged by a number of questions. The big question that weaves through everything else, echoing the great commandment, and which has reverberated all through the story of humanity is this: What is Love? Iñigo also places this question very prominently right at the end of the Exercises, challenging us to ponder its depths as our lives move on. He calls his challenge the *Contemplatio ad Amorem*, calling us to consider how we might love God and each other with a love that reflects the divine.

A key tenet of Ignatian wisdom and of Gospel truth is that love reveals itself in action more than in words. The word 'love' has been seriously devalued in contemporary society. We use it loosely, and sometimes thoughtlessly, to express affection or romantic feelings, or even a preference for a particular food or fashion trend. The real deal is far more demanding. Psychiatrist and author M. Scott Peck provides an invaluable key to understanding divine love when he asserts, 'Love is not an emotion. Love is a decision.' Or in the words of the English writer Samuel Johnson, 'Kindness is in our power, even when fondness is not.'

This insight tells us that, however we may be feeling, we can choose, in every situation, to do the more loving thing, to act and behave in a kind and loving manner. This choice, this decision, doesn't depend on our emotional state at the time and Jesus tells us plainly that it applies to ourselves, our neighbours, colleagues, friends, strangers, and, crucially, even our enemies.

There are no exceptions, because God is the *one* in whom *all* have their being. To love God, as the first commandment requires, is to choose to act lovingly not only to each other, but to our living planet and all the life it sustains. We cannot claim to love God if we behave unlovingly to any part of God's creation. Jesus also calls us to be especially aware of the demands of love in the way we relate to the poorest among us, the marginalised, the oppressed, the voiceless, the helpless and the exploited.

Love, it is clear, is the answer to every question we have considered during this retreat. Love asks us to live from our deeper 'God-Centre' and not from our shallow and self-focused ego-centre. It is Love that invites us to launch our lives into the deeper waters and follow Jesus through the events of his earthly ministry, modelling our own lives and values on his. Love is the heartbeat of the challenge of discernment, prompting us to make choices that reflect the very best we can be. Love asks of us that we let go of all that is impeding our soul's journey, moving forward with empty hands so that we are free to receive all the graces that God longs to give us. It is Love that calls us, and empowers us, to make the journey into darkness and death alongside Jesus in Holy Week, remembering that in our world with all its perils, especially for the poorest, the marginalised, and the lost, *every* week is Holy Week. And it is Love who stands on the shore, showing us that the treasure we long for may be in the place we never thought to look. It is Love who invites us to share breakfast, as a new beginning dawns for humankind and for all creation.

Do we have faith? Not just creedal believing, but *trust*? Do we believe and trust that, by the grace of God, we can grow back better from the adversity we face?

Do we have hope? I think we do, even though we sometimes feel we are hanging onto it by a slender thread.

'But the greatest of these is love.' Dare we ask for the grace to choose love, and to keep on asking ourselves: *What is love asking of me right now?*

Talk to God

As you travel on, try applying this question to any situation in which you find yourself: What is the more loving thing to do next? There are no easy answers. Sometimes love will ask us to intervene, perhaps to challenge an injustice; sometimes it will ask us to stand back and leave another person free to discover their own way forward. Love will sometimes be tender, comforting the afflicted, and sometimes it will be tough, refusing to allow ourselves or others to be manipulated or exploited. Love may come easily as we support our loved ones, or it may be the hardest task imaginable as we try to be alongside someone who has hurt us or those we love.

God's love is continually being poured out into all creation. How does the love we claim to have for God reveal itself in a corresponding love for our planet and all her life forms? How can we express this love in practical ways?

Look back over your journal or any notes you have made during the retreat. What graces do you feel you have been given as you have made this journey of prayer? What has changed in your life, your heart and your faith since Ash Wednesday? How will you sustain this growth and respond in practical ways to what you have learned?

Two new graduates, standing on the dais at their graduation ceremony, were asked by the Dean, 'What are you going to do next?' One announced the intention of making a world-changing breakthrough in medical science. The other replied 'I am going to turn left and walk very carefully down these three steps.' Each of them had grasped half the truth. We are pilgrims of God, called and empowered to dream big, big dreams for the greater good of all creation, and make them real on planet Earth. But we make them real by attending carefully to the next three steps we take, our next three conversations, interactions or choices, asking moment by moment: *What is Love asking me to do next?*

May God bless and guide all our steps, from this day forward, until God's kingdom is fully birthed on Earth, as it is in heaven. Amen.

EASTER

Easter

Introduction to Easter

The Easter season is itself the great season of encounter, of dialogue, as different New Testament figures come to faith in Jesus risen from the dead. An ancient Easter greeting found especially in the ancient churches of the East goes like this: Christ is risen, he is truly risen! We need to hear this acclamation now more than ever before, for it announces something momentous: Evil, death and destruction are not the final word on each of us or on our lives or on our world, in spite of evidence to the contrary. This conviction is grounded in the proclamation of Christ risen, victorious over death, setting us free even from the fear of death itself. In the elevated vision of Gerard Manley Hopkins SJ,

> I am all at once what Christ is,
> since he was what I am, and
> This Jack, joke, poor potsherd,
> patch, matchwood, immortal diamond,
> Is immortal diamond.

This is so good, so exactly what we need to hear as 'hearers of the word', it has to be true!

Kieran J. O'Mahony OSA,
Hearers of the Word: Easter & Pentecost, Year A

Easter Reflections

The Resurrection

Icons of Christ at the well with the Samaritan woman usually show him wearing a blue mantle over a red robe. Red signifies his humanity, the colour of the reddish earth from which Adam was made (Genesis 25:25). His humanity is in essence with his divinity, generally represented as blue, sometimes using crushed lapis lazuli, a most expensive mineral, at that time mined only in Afghanistan. Often, in the images of this scene, the blue colour has faded, as though in harmony with the simple human need of water that Jesus has. There is little difference between the red and the blue in this image, as though the humanity is showing through in greater clarity. As well as symbolising life, blood, passion and love in iconography in general, red has also come to symbolise the life-blood of Christ, poured out for us. The Resurrection, too, is associated with red to proclaim Christ's victory of life over death. The iconographer invites us to also contemplate the resurrection of this woman, and the offer of eternal life to all people, extending beyond the Jewish people—although we know that God's promise to them is never rescinded and God's relationship with them remains true for all time.

Magdalen Lawler SND,
Well of Living Water: Jesus and the Samaritan Woman

Mary Magdalene and the Gardener

The story mentions that Mary turned around twice: first when she faced into the tomb, and the Gardener [Jesus], standing behind her, asked why she was weeping. She turned to ask him her own question about where he had put the body. Then she must have turned back towards the tomb again, because we are told that when he spoke her name she turned back to him a second time and embraced his feet. The image may be stressing that Mary turned away from the grave, from death, towards life—incredible new life. In part this is about one man being alive instead of dead, but it is also about much more than that. After having spoken her name, the Gardener said something more. Something that seems even more out of place than his question to Mary at the grave, 'Why are you crying?' He said, 'Do not cling to me.' What did he expect her to do? He knew how much she loved him. He knew that she had suffered brutally watching his suffering and death. Now that he had spoken her name, thereby transforming darkness and despair into incredible hope, what did he expect her to do? Yet he said, 'Do not cling to me.'

The reason that the Gardener told her not to cling to him was that he had not yet gone back to his Father. Speaking her name meant that he had overcome death, that he was alive. But this did not mean that everything would go back to what it had been before his death. This pointed to a reality that was difficult: his death had changed their relationship. But it pointed to something else that was even more important: his death had not ended their relationship. In fact, by the power of his Spirit, his death was going to deepen their relationship in ways that she could not imagine.

Brian Lennon SJ,
Mary Magdalene and the Gardener

The Road to Emmaus

The journey of the two disciples away from Jerusalem is a very human journey. As they walked together they carried the burden of loss. The one to whom they had given their lives and who was the source of their hope had been cruelly put to death. The sense of loss in their hearts was visible on their faces, 'their faces downcast'. We have all travelled that sad journey of loss at one time or another. In times of war, whole nations travel it together. Unknown to the two disciples, the one in whom they had put their hopes was now journeying with them, prompting them to tell the story of their loss, inviting them to listen to a bigger, more hopeful, story contained in the Scriptures, a story that ended in glory, not death. The words of the stranger left the hearts of the disciples burning within them. When they reached their destination and the stranger made to go on, they didn't want to let him go. He accepted their invitation to share their table and it was at table that they recognised him in the breaking of bread, the early Church's term for the Eucharist. The moment when the eyes of the disciples were opened in recognition of the stranger was also the moment when he vanished from their sight. Yet they now knew that Jesus was powerfully alive, present in the Scriptures, in the Eucharist and in the community of believers.

The sad journey out of the city of Jerusalem now gave way to a joyful journey back to the city to share this Easter good news. As they shared their good news with their companions, they heard back from them the same good news, 'Yes, it is true. The Lord has risen and has appeared to Simon.' This is our good news too. The risen Lord journeys with us in our times of loss and sadness. He is present to us in his word, in the Eucharist, in the community of believers, the Church. The Lord's presence to us empowers us to be present to each other in the same life-giving way that he was present to the two disciples on the road to Emmaus. This is how Peter and John were present to the man crippled from birth in the first reading. The risen Lord, working through them, empowered the man to walk, just as the risen Lord empowered the two disciples to journey back to the other disciples in joyful hope. The Lord wants to work through each one of us to enable others to walk with renewed hope and life in their hearts.

Martin Hogan,
Your Word Is a Lamp on My Path

On Earth We Are Christ's Body

I asked a woman once if Johnny was in the house. She pointed at a chair and said, 'If he was here he would be there.' He never moved far! Jesus—he is here and there. The risen Lord has moved on, but he has not fully left us. His Spirit dwells in us.

The one who came to earth has now gone back to heaven, bringing with him all that is human. His body—the man of heaven and the God of earth—is now the Church, and that's us.

Before we are of any denomination or group, we are Christ's. We are baptised into the Church of Christ; we live out our faith in different denominations. Today is the feast of the whole Church—we begin in him and end in him, like the Alpha and Omega, the beginning and the end, on the paschal candle. Our faith is renewed through living with Jesus—we are partners in our mission. Our faith is also renewed in reading and praying the Gospel each day.

On earth we are his body, with all our strengths and weaknesses, goodness and sin. Icons have Jesus smiling as he reaches heaven, smiling on us and living through us. Next Sunday, we will prepare for the way he is with us now: in the Spirit. Where the qualities of the Spirit are alive, he is alive and well among us.

Donal Neary SJ,
Gospel Reflections for Sundays of Year A

Pentecost

The disciples are hiding behind locked doors. The life and ministry of Jesus have come to a brutal end. They have witnessed the empty tomb, and Mary Magdalene has seen Jesus, but the other disciples have not, yet. Could it be that they are sceptical of Mary's account? Their fear, while natural, has the sense of an ending, a disappointment. It is into this closed-off situation that Jesus comes, bringing hope and newness, literally 'breathing' new life. His act of breathing the Holy Spirit on the disciples mirrors God breathing life into Adam and Ezekiel; it is breath that gives and sustains life. In fact, the Greek (*pneuma*) and Hebrew (*ruach*) words for 'spirit' can also be translated as 'breath'. It is this breath that God breathes into each and every one of us, continually creating us anew.

Jesus' first word to the disciples is *Shalom*: peace. The risen Jesus brings a blessing and a peace that are life-giving. The disciples now have the Spirit of God in their midst, and this Spirit will guide how they relate with each other. Experiencing the power of God's love, peace and mercy, they are called to share this with one another and with the world. Guided by these values from within, we are called to build communities of love and peace. We are all created by God, breathed into life, equally loved and equally valued whatever our background, position in life, ethnicity, sexuality. The Spirit is not confined to any time or place or people, but dwells in everyone and is present in every culture and age. How can this truth be lived out in our actions, individually and as community, parish, church? When peace and love replace fear, new possibilities are opened up, we embrace our differences and trust that the Spirit is at work.

Tríona Doherty and Jane Mellet,
The Deep End: A Journey with the Sunday Gospels in the Year of Mark

PRAYERS

Ignatian Prayers

Examen

The daily Examen is a prayer that Ignatius gave great importance to. If all prayers during the course of the day were to be missed, the Examen was the only one that must never be missed, Ignatius told his companions. Such were the benefits that Ignatius found in this simple but profound prayer. The Examen is a review of your day and has five parts to it.

This is a version of the five-step daily Examen that Ignatius practiced:

1. Become aware of God's presence.
2. Review the day with gratitude.
3. How did I respond/how did I feel?
4. Choose one feature of the day and pray from it.
5. Look towards tomorrow.

Looking back over our day for about 5/10 minutes helps us to get in touch with where God was and where God is leading us. Ignatius describes this as 'my eyes were opened a little' as he slowly began to see how God loved him and where he was being guided in specific ways during the day. This is what we are also invited to do as we review our day. When we see how we are loved by God and can experience it then everything changes. Ignatius believed this short practice of prayer was a gift from God.

Step 1: Become aware of God's presence with you now.
As when praying with Sacred Space, try to become aware of God's presence: I remind myself that in these moments, God is gazing on me with deep and unconditional love and holding me in being. I pause and think of this.

Step 2: Review your day with gratitude.
Looking back over the course of your day, what are you grateful for? Try to be concrete about the things you are thankful for—maybe your family, job, good health, a chat with a friend, happy memories, a walk in nature, the beauty of creation. Can you notice where God was present in all this? Can you see the gifts God has given this day? Even if the day was really difficult, is there something you are thankful for?

Step 3: How did I respond to the moments of my day/how did I feel?
Was I able to notice God's promptings during the moments of the day I have just recalled? Did I respond to people and situations in a good way or was it not so good? Did my heart feel warm and full or was it discouraged, with little energy? Did God feel close or far

away during my day? Did my responses help to build the relationships, both human and divine, in my life? If things didn't go too well today, remember how we are loved and held by God in all our brokenness and vulnerability. As we ask forgiveness, we are showered with love, healing and the grace to move forward.

Step 4: Choose one feature from the day and pray from it.

Was there one encounter/situation/person that was particularly positive or challenging for me today? Bring this time to God now and talk openly and freely about it and how it was for you. Trust that God is interested in this and offers love, peace and healing to you.

Step 5: Look towards tomorrow.

As you come to the end of your prayer from today, look ahead to tomorrow and invite God to be with you in all that the day will bring. If there is something particular that you have planned—a meeting, appointment, trip or maybe another day just by yourself—ask God to be with you in it. Our God is a God of relationship. What's important to us, is important to God. As in the words spoken to Jeremiah 31:3: 'I have loved you with an everlasting love; therefore I have continued my faithfulness to you.'

Suscipe (Prayer of St Ignatius of Loyola)

Take, Lord, and receive all my liberty,
my memory, my understanding,
and my entire will,
all I have and call my own.

You have given all to me.
To you, Lord, I return it.

Everything is yours; do with it what you will.
Give me only your love and your grace,
that is enough for me.

———

O Deus Ego Amo Te
(Prayer of St Francis Xavier,
trans. Gerard Manley Hopkins SJ)

O God, I love thee, I love thee—
Not out of hope of heaven for me
Nor fearing not to love and be
In the everlasting burning.
Thou, thou, my Jesus, after me
Didst reach thine arms out dying,
For my sake sufferedst nails, and lance,
Mocked and marred countenance,
Sorrows passing number,
Sweat and care and cumber,
Yea and death, and this for me,

And thou couldst see me sinning:
Then I, why should not I love thee,
Jesu, so much in love with me?
Not for heaven's sake; not to be
Out of hell by loving thee;
Not for any gains I see;
But just the way that thou didst me
I do love and I will love thee:
What must I love thee, Lord, for then?—
For being my king and God. Amen.

———

The St Francis Xavier Novena Prayer

O most kind and loving saint, in union with you I
    adore the
Divine Majesty. The remembrance of the favours
    with which
God blessed you during life, and of your glory
    after death,
fills me with joy; and I unite with you in offering
    to God my
humble tribute of thanksgiving and of praise.

I implore of you to secure for me, through your
    powerful
intercession, the all-important blessing of living
    and dying

in the state of grace. I also beseech you to obtain
for me
the favour I ask in this Novena
(here mention the favour to be asked for),
but if what I ask is not for the glory of God
or for the good of my soul, obtain for me what is
most
conducive to both. Amen.

'Thou art indeed just, Lord, if I contend'
(Poem of Gerard Manley Hopkins SJ)

Thou art indeed just, Lord, if I contend
With thee; but, sir, so what I plead is just.
Why do sinners' ways prosper? and why must
Disappointment all I endeavour end?
Wert thou my enemy, O thou my friend,
How wouldst thou worse, I wonder, than thou dost
Defeat, thwart me? Oh, the sots and thralls of lust
Do in spare hours more thrive than I that spend,
Sir, life upon thy cause. See, banks and brakes
Now, leavèd how thick! lacèd they are again
With fretty chervil, look, and fresh wind shakes
Them; birds build—but not I build; no, but strain,
Time's eunuch, and not breed one work that wakes.
Mine, O thou lord of life, send my roots rain.

Prayer in Time of Trial
(Prayer of Willie Doyle SJ)

Oh Master! I come to your feet to tell you all.

I have buried my dead.

I have lost what can never be restored to me in this
world.

I have come from the grave with half myself buried
there.

I have come back to a life with all its meaning gone
from it—

a life without joy, interest, anything to which my
soul responds—

a dreary waste stretching before me that I must
cross alone.

Where shall I turn for courage and for strength?

Where but to you, to whom the disciples of John
turned in their desolation?

Open to me your arms and your heart.

Listen to me tenderly whilst I tell you all my
trouble.

Speak to my soul and calm and strengthen it.

Make up to me for what you have taken away.

And if you ask me what compensation I desire, I
answer:

'None other than thyself, O Lord.'

In the Hands of God
(Prayer of Pedro Arrupe SJ)

More than ever I find myself in the hands of God.
This is what I have wanted all my life from my youth.
But now there is a difference;
the initiative is entirely with God.

It is indeed a profound spiritual experience
to know and feel myself so totally in God's hands.

Falling in Love with God
(Prayer of Joseph Whelan SJ)

Nothing is more practical than finding God,
that is, than falling in love in a quite absolute,
    final way.
What you are in love with,
what seizes your imagination,
will affect everything.
It will decide what will get you out of bed in the
    morning,
what you do with your evenings,
how you spend your weekends,
what you read, whom you know, what breaks your
    heart,
and what amazes you with joy and gratitude.
Fall in love, stay in love, and it will decide
    everything!

Contemporary Prayers by Irish Jesuits

An Easter Prayer
by Brendan McManus SJ

Lord, help me still this feverish mind,
Give me peace that I may rest awhile
Invite me into your love, call me by name,
let me linger at your house like the Emmaus disciples.

Turn my heart towards the mystery of your love,
poured out for me personally on the Cross,
Let me realise the wonder of this gift to me,
Insulate me in your hope and courage.

I need to believe that your Son has known my
    struggles,
I need to know I am not alone but held,
I need to believe in your new life and a new dawn.
Instil the light of your resurrection instead of this
    fear.

You knew the full dark tomb
Lived through death and despair
Release me from my crippling fears and doubts,
Illuminate even the darkest night with your love.

Cradle me from the depths of despair,
Protect me from the inner corrosion of spirit,
Create a new heart in me despite everything,
Fill this heart full of gratitude and joy.

Help me to see the signs of resurrection everywhere,
Give me the eyes to see the beauty of creation,
To see everything as a gift,
To see your presence in those around me.

Lord, bring me back to life,
Let me live in your love always,
Hold me close to your heart.
Bring me home, I pray. Amen.

———

A Eucharistic Prayer
by Niall Leahy SJ

*First I invite people to place their hand on their heart
and to close their eyes. Then I lead them as follows,
pausing after each line.*

Jesus, thank you for giving yourself to me in the
    Eucharist.
I welcome you into my body,
I welcome you into my heart,
and I welcome you, Lord, into my life.
May my heart always be close to yours, Lord,
and may your heart always be close to mine.

———

A Synodal Prayer
by Gerry O'Hanlon SJ

Lord Jesus,

We had hoped . . .

The Bishop of Rome told us that if we walked together, if we spoke honestly and openly, if we listened patiently and generously, then you would join us and your Spirit would show us the way.

But all we seemed to hear was the pain of those we in our Church had hurt: the open wound of abuse, the humiliation and dishonouring of women, our insensitivity to those who could not share or agree with teaching on sexuality and gender.

We sensed our impotence in the face of those who had no or little faith, the young people who walked away from us with indifference, our weak efforts to stem the ravaging of our planet, to bring peace instead of war to our troubled world, to provide shelter and welcome to migrants, to be on the side of the poor in our so unequal world.

And so, we were downcast, we had no energy, we fought among ourselves. Something prevented us from recognising you walking along beside us.

Until . . .

You gathered us in the upper room of the Sheraton Hotel in Athlone and amidst all the fear and gloom we sensed your presence in the breaking of the Word, your Spirit afterwards out on the rolling hills of Clonmacnoise, by the banks of the river Shannon.

And our hearts burned within us . . .

And we understood that your peace surpasses all human understanding, that your strength was present in the earthenware jars of our weakness, that you were true to your word, and that you were the hope of our world.

And we understood that our joy, our radiance, would not always shine so brightly, that our present consolation was strength to look back on, to remember, to keep us going when we once again began to lose heart and lost sight of your walking along beside us.

Lord we believe, help our unbelief.

Come Lord Jesus. Amen.

Daily Prayers
by Donal Neary SJ

In the morning . . .
May you come among us each day.
Lord God, open our hearts to your love.
Let us share that love among those we love,
care for and meet each day.
May your love be upon us O Lord.
We place all our hope in you.
    Amen.

You have made this day, O Lord;
may I spend it well in your service:
praying at all times,
serving your people, who I meet this day,
with love and care.
    Amen.

Holy Spirit, make my heart open to the word of
    God,
make my heart open to goodness,
make my heart open to the beauty of God every day.
    Amen.

During the day . . .
Come, Lord Jesus, child of the earth, child of God.
Come into our world of joy and sorrow.
Stay with us always now and at the hour of our
    death.
    Amen.

Be with me Lord when I need strength and healing
    in my life;
Be with your people so that we follow you in
    loving service.
Be with our world in its need for your mercy and
    your care.
    Amen.

At night . . .
For what was good in today, I thank you O Lord.
For what was difficult I ask your help. Look after
all whom I met today, especially any who urgently
need my prayers. Give me peace this night and bring
peace to our world.
    Amen.

Lord, I entrust myself to your loving care this night.
I rest in the assurance of your promises for me.
May I awaken to a new day with faith hope and joy
knowing that you are always with me.
    Amen.

Prayer of the Lonely Crown
by Edmond Grace SJ

I

Why would you hide your face from me?
I know it's there.
Why do you hide it unrelentingly?
Why do you let me drag myself around,
while others come to stop and stare
at the angry faith which pulls me down?

How can I know what I have not seen?
How can your love remain untouched?
How can the unheard tune be found?
My longing has fretfully clutched
at the air and lifted the lonely crown.

Can you hear the buried scream
in these mangled feet which have journeyed far?
How can they turn from you and walk away
when my shoulders sag and the hour is late?

I will soon be summoned to a feast
where every bruise and twisted bone and scar
will dance and on that day,
from the greatest to the least,
all will feed on your sweet tenderness.

What if you decided not to wait?
What if you raised your hand to bless

me here and now amid the swirling sands
of time and passers-by would recognise
the easy voice and laughing eyes
and the soft contented sigh
of fearless age at peace with death?

You know my longing and my ache.
Reach into my tortured hope and take
these strangled prayers into your open hands.
Touch them with your fingers and your breath
and let them fly.

II

My feet have always known this place.
Each passing day I knock on the door
of your crumbling shelter. Nothing is heard.

Behind the fragile stones your warlike face
is watching the world with a troubled frown
as you weigh your thoughts and stand before
the dark disturbing possibilities.

You call my name with tight lipped welcomings
and side by side we stand. You proffer your
    preferred
and proudly gilded memories
and lead me to your lonely crown.

I want to take your hand and toss your hair
but you withdraw to scowling lands of hate.
You hide among the sad important things
and so I calmly wait
until your stumbling journey ends
and our eyes will meet in the cheerful air.

We will laugh out loud like long-lost friends.